The Amazing Women of the Bible:
Twelve Character Studies

by Wilson Adams

Lesson 1
The Amazing Women of the Bible
Introduction

The greatest question facing our study is this: how do you limit the number of women God used to only a select few? There are certainly many more than those included here. From beginning to end of the biblical narrative, God used a vast assortment of extraordinary women through whom He weaved a plan for man's redemption. In fact, the salvation story would be impossible without them.

We are constantly encouraged by their lives and their struggles. And we are reminded again and again that the God of Abraham, Isaac, and Jacob was equally the God of Sarah, Rebekah, and Rachel. He is, after all, the God of each generation and gender. Paul spoke to this in Galatians 3:28—"There is neither Jew nor Greek, there is neither slave nor free man, there is neither male nor female; for you are all one in Christ Jesus."

The amazing women of the Bible were, indeed, amazing. Not because they were somehow different than women of today (the exception being Eve—who was born fully adult, married as an adult new-born, and had no other of her gender with whom to share her struggles, etc.), but "amazing" in the sense that each had a life-changing encounter with a holy God who used them providentially to change the lives of others.

Our goal is simple: to share their stories and their faith; to imitate their godliness and to learn from their lives. Such a study will enrich anyone (male or female) who dares to pull back the curtain of Holy Writ and view the stories of *The Amazing Women of the Bible.*

I. The Biblical Model—the Exaltation of Women.

One of the unique features of the Bible (contrary to the way most are led to believe) is the way Scripture exalts women. Rather than demeaning or belittling them, the Bible presents them in the most positive of lights—ennobling their roles in God's plan, acknowledging their influence over others, and exalting the virtues of their God-given femininity and creativity. Anyone arguing otherwise does so from a position of ignorance (they haven't read the Bible) or prejudice (they have relied upon the social spin of feminists). Certainly there are roles and responsibilities the Creator has given to each gender—but none of those roles and responsibilities has to do with equality of personhood. Even in the home where the husband is given leadership, Peter makes sure we understand that we are "fellow heirs of the grace of life" (1 Peter 3:7). He also warns that any man who fails to grasp that truth will find a barrier to his own relationship with God (v. 7b).

A. **The Biblical model.** From the first chapter in Genesis we learn that both men and women bear the stamp of God's image (v. 27). Genesis 5:1–2 declares further that God "created them male and female, and He blessed them and named them." From then on and throughout the biblical narrative women are never seen as slaves or "things," but as a cherished creation of God. In fact, Moses walked down from the lofty heights of Sinai with a declaration cut in stone: "Honor your father and your mother" (Exodus 20:12). Such was revolutionary in a pagan world where men ruled with an iron fist.

1. Yes, there are God-appointed roles of distinction. For example,

• Women are unique in their role of childbearing—a fact of anatomy and biology that no amount of social engineering can change. Two men cannot bear a child. Two women cannot bear a child. God's plan for human reproduction is clear. Equally so, it has always been God's plan that children produced by male and female, be brought up beneath the protected roof of the marital male/female relationship (Genesis 2:24; Matthew 19:4–6).

- The Bible establishes proper order for the family (Ephesians 5:23). The role of leadership, protector, and provider is given to the man and illustrated throughout Scripture.
- The New Testament shows that leadership roles in the local church are given to the man. From the appointment of the Twelve (men) to the designation that local church elders be men (1 Timothy 3:1); from the work of preaching to leading the assembly in other ways (1 Corinthians 14:34–35), women are not to take roles of leadership. Scripture is especially clear about these roles, responsibilities, and restrictions.

2. On the other hand, the Bible nowhere marginalizes women and presents them as less in gender importance.

- How can anyone read Ephesians 5:22–33 (where sacred marriage is compared to the sacred relationship between Christ and His church) and not understand that the woman is to be loved and cherished for the person God made her to be?
- The exaltation of the virtuous woman (Proverbs 31) is without equal.
- The Genesis stories of the patriarchs (Abraham, Isaac, Jacob) give equal space to the stories and struggles of their wives (Sarah, Rebekah, and Rachel).
- Miriam (Moses' sister) played a key role in God's providence and became a prophetess and song writer.
- Deborah was a judge.
- Rahab overcame a closet full of skeletons to become a heroine of faith (Hebrews 11:31) while appearing in the genealogy of Jesus (Matthew 1:5).

- And then there is Esther—the little orphaned girl who became queen of her people. Her story and God's hand of providence upon her life is both amazing and inspiring.
- In the book of Proverbs, "wisdom" is personified as a woman.
- The New Testament church is picture-painted as the "bride" of Christ.
- In a name-calling list of brethren who had touched the life of Paul (Romans 16), the majority are women.

3. The above bullet-points are only that—and to the list could be added dozens more. The exaltation of women, however, is woefully missing in other cultures.

B. **The Roman empire.** Pagan cultures treated women with no more dignity than a dog. Greek philosophers taught that women were inferior to men, regarded them as chattel property, and presented them in mythology as mere sex objects. Religious ceremonies may have designated them as "priestesses," but in actuality they were nothing more than prostitutes. And then came Christianity:

1. Jesus elevated women to unprecedented heights. It is noted that many of the early supporters of Jesus' preaching were women (Luke 8:1–3). The first recorded disclosure of His identity as Messiah was made to a woman (John 4:25–26). Jesus blessed their children, raised their dead, and refused to participate in first century chauvinism when they brought to Him only the "woman" caught in adultery (John 8:3–11).

2. It was the same in the days of the early church. From the example of Dorcas (Acts 9:36–42) to the hospitality of John Mark's mother (12:12), from the kindness of Lydia (Acts 16:14–15) to the sacrifices of Aquilla and Priscilla—"and the church meeting in their house" (1 Corinthians 16:19)—Christianity lifted women from the debauchery that accompanied them in paganism.

3. It was only after Emperor Constantine became favorable to Christianity that women were given legal status and protection by Rome. A philandering husband could no longer treat his wife any way he wished. Thus everywhere the gospel went, it elevated women to their God-honored place. Where the gospel was refused, however, the status of women declined.

C. **The Islamic world.** Anyone who would question the last affirmation need look no further than Islam. The Koran teaches that women exist for the purpose of serving men to the point that if a wife is disobedient, she may be beaten. Under Sharia law, women are not equal. Muslim men may have up to four wives and if he should become unhappy with any of them, he may divorce her with three words spoken three times: "I divorce you." At that point all the children and property belong to the man.

1. Child marriages are common throughout the Islamic world. In Iran, the legal age of marriage for girls is *nine.* In Afghanistan the average girl is married by age thirteen.

2. The Koran teaches that a husband may beat his wife as a third stage of discipline (#1: verbal warning, #2: banishment to the bedroom). FYI: Muslim men are seldom convicted in rape cases. In the majority of cases, it is the woman who is jailed and sometimes stoned.

3. This is not the world of yesterday; it is the world of today in Muslim cultures. Guess what is coming to America?

D. **Feminism.** The feminist movement demeans women because it devalues femininity (a God-given quality) and ridicules the roles of a loving wife and nurturing mother. The Creator gave unique distinctions to each gender. It's true physically, but also true emotionally and chemically. And while Christianity values those distinctions, the message of feminism is that there is nothing amazing about women. They are wrong.

II. Yes, They Are Amazing!

The Bible women are not amazing because of their beauty or their career, but because of their character (1 Peter 3:3–4). Never does the Bible discount a woman's intellect, degrade her ability, or discourage the right use of her God-given talents. I hope you enjoy these studies and, above all, I hope you will learn that it is their faithfulness to God that is their lasting legacy. May these women challenge, motivate, and inspire you to be all that God made you to be.

Discussion Questions
Prompting Additional Insight

1. Why do you think this study is valuable in the context of our culture? *So many have stopped searching the Bible. Need to know what God intended for women.*

2. Name a woman from both the Old and New Testaments that you admire and who gives you encouragement. Discuss why she is your choice. *Esther – she was loyal to her people even in danger. Dorcas – she glorified God by her works.*

3. What do we learn from the following passages about gender equality?
   —Genesis 1:27 *Both of us were made in God's image.*
   —Galatians 3:28 *Everyone is "one" in Christ Jesus.*
   —1 Peter 3:7 *We are joint heirs*

4. How can we teach our girls to have greater appreciation for the honorable roles of marriage and motherhood in the face of a culture that often belittles both?
   – example
   – Bible study
   –

5. According to Exodus 20:12, who is to receive honor in the home?

Mom & dad

6. Do the God-given roles of distinction for male and female in both the home and the church (male leadership) have anything to do with equality of personhood? *no. IT Takes BoTH to make a strong family*

   Follow-up: Christians in the local church are to submit themselves to those appointed as local church shepherds (Hebrews 13:17). Does this principle of submission mean the rest of us are less in the eyes of God than are they? Submission doesn't mean inequality; it does mean that we understand the roles and responsibilities given to different ones. Discuss.

7. Christianity clashed with culture—then and now. In the first century, women were regarded as mere property or viewed as sex objects. In what ways are women seen or promoted similarly today? *TV*

8. What amazed the disciples in John 4:27—and why?

Jesus tacked w/ a woman

9. Western feminists often make odd assertions. One feminist went so far as to defend Islam by saying, "Christianity [in contrast to Islam] perpetuates sexism." Her statement proves that she knows little about Christianity or Islam. Google Islam and their treatment of women and discuss your findings.

10. According to Proverbs 31:30, what will cause a woman to be praised? *one who fears the Lord.*

Lesson 2

The Amazing Story of Eve

Genesis 1–4

Then the Lord God said, "It is not good for the man to be alone;
I will make a helper suitable for him."
—Genesis 2:18—

What immediately comes to your mind when you hear the name Eve?

1. The first woman
2. The last living being created
3. The youngest bride ever
4. The crowning jewel of creation
5. I thought about her during the piercing pains of childbirth

Scripture says that Adam was made from "the dust of the ground" (Genesis 2:7). And Eve? Someone said, If God made Adam from a handful of dirt, then God made Eve from a handful of Adam. True. And to that we may add: He saved the best for last!

The creation of woman was the zenith of all creation, the finishing touch. Interestingly enough, the Bible gives no physical description of Eve (her literal Hebrew name was *Ishshah* until 3:20), but we can only imagine that she was beautiful and adorned with an equal amount of inner beauty which is "precious in the sight of God" (1 Peter 3:3–4).

She is called "the mother of all living" (3:20) and played a major role in the story of Scripture and the plan for human redemption. Oddly enough, her name is used only four times (twice in the Old Testament and twice in the New—2 Corinthians 11:3; 1 Timothy 2:13).

We don't know what she looked like. We don't know how long she lived. We don't know where and how she died.

However, what we do know about her is *amazing!*

I. Her Creation—Genesis 2:20–25.
   A. **Sleep and surgery!** Adam is anesthetized ("So the Lord caused a deep sleep to fall upon the man"), his side opened, a rib removed, and the incision closed. The skilled Surgeon took a bone Adam would not miss and made the one being he had missed—"a helper suitable for him" (v. 20). By God's grace and design, He made the perfect counterpart for the man. Adam lost a rib and gained a loving life-companion. Finally, Eden had become "paradise."
      1. Was it love at first sight? One thing was for sure, the moment he saw her (a definite *"Aha!"* moment), he knew. It wasn't as if there were other "fish in the sea." His first words capture a profound sense of wonder, delight, and complete satisfaction. This is now bone of my bones and flesh of my flesh . . . Adam found the one who had been missing.
   B. **Truths about womanhood from Eve:**
      1. Her fundamental equality with Adam. "She was taken out of man." They shared the same essential nature. She was not made inferior to him but made from him.
      2. The ideal union of marriage. When Jesus returned to the garden wedding (Matthew 19:4–6), He did so to prove that the first marriage set the precedent for all marriages (Genesis 2:24–25).
      3. An illustration of the meaning of marriage. This was not just a physical thing, but a union of heart and soul. Perhaps the Puritan author, Matthew Henry, says it best: "She was made of a rib out of the side of Adam; not made out of his head to rule over him, nor out of his feet to be trampled upon by him, but out of his side to be equal with him, under his arm to be protected, and near his heart to be loved."

4. The God-designed role of women. Although equal in being and essence, each of the genders had distinct roles. We learn in 1 Corinthians 11:8–9, 12:
   - Adam was created first, then Eve
   - Adam was the head, Eve the helper
   - Adam would be father, provider, protector, leader; Eve would be mother, comforter, nurturer, helper

   God designed each with different functions to fit their uniqueness. The feminist movement of our times seeks to deny the obvious. We are equal, but we are different. And the Creator gave specific gender roles to each.

C. **Mutual partnership.** When both genders embrace God's purpose, both are happier and the family is stronger. The question has been asked: How could she subordinate herself to his leadership and still be his equal? 1 Corinthians 11:3 is the answer.

   1. All three persons of Deity are equal, yet each took on different roles. For example, the Bible shows that the Son became subordinate to the Father. Now if three can have different roles yet still be one (equal), certainly two can have different roles yet still be one.

   2. Adam and Eve represent a true picture of what God expects for marriage and the roles each are to fulfill.

II. Tempted!

A. The tempter wasted no time sabotaging the first family (3:1–7). His opening line to her is revealing, "Indeed, has God said, 'You shall not eat from any tree of the garden'?" First, his words dripped with sarcasm. Second, he masterfully twisted what God said. God never said what Satan quoted. The Creator said they could eat freely "from any tree in the garden, except . . . " (2:16–17). Later, Jesus reminds us that Satan is a liar and "the father of lies" (John 8:44). It continues to be his modus operandi—questioning God, raising doubt, insinuating suspicion, etc. He lied that day, and he continues to lie to this day.

1. Rather than walking away, Eve entertains the tempter and repeats God's prohibition (vv. 2–3). It is then that Satan contradicts God (vv. 4-5).

2. Yes, in succumbing to the temptation her eyes would be opened, but in a way she did not understand. Eating the forbidden fruit would not make Eve more like God as much as it would make her more like Satan—fallen, corrupt, and condemned.

B. Eve gave in, ate, and handed the same to her husband (v. 6). There seemed to be no sense of hesitation on her part, nor upon his. Sin had entered the world.

III. Her Humiliation.

A. **The fallout.** Satan was right about one thing: she would know "good and evil" seeing that she had become a willing participant in the latter. Innocence gone, the first couple immediately concocted a human scheme to cover their sin (v. 7). It failed. Then again, every human attempt to cover sin will ultimately fail. Masking guilt doesn't make it go away.

1. What follows is predictable (3:8–13). Before, they enjoyed the presence of God. Now, they fear Him.

2. It is interesting that God addresses Adam first. Why? Because God made him the leader. Note that God gave to each the opportunity to confess. Instead of confessing, each engaged in blame-shifting. "The woman whom You gave to be with me, she gave me from the tree, and I ate" (v. 12). It's all her fault! In fact, Adam twists it to make it God's fault!

3. Eve sought equal justification for her sin (v. 13). *"The serpent deceived me."* That was true. It did not, however, justify her disobedience. "Each one is tempted when he is carried away and enticed by his own lust," (James 1:14).

No matter the means Satan uses, the decision to sin is always our own.

4. *Note:* God makes no argument nor does He entertain any dialogue. In fact, our excuses today are no better at concealing our guilt than fig leaves covered theirs. You cannot hide or deceive Him (Galatians 6:7).

B. **The Curse, 3:14–19.** God issues a comprehensive curse on the serpent, the woman, and the man. Adam's life would change significantly. So would hers. Eve and every woman after her would find their pain multiplied in childbirth and an opened door for enhanced struggles between husbands and wives and their respective roles.

1. Sin carries consequences. It always does. Yet even in the curse, there was grace. First, although Adam and Eve were banished from the Garden of Eden, they were not destroyed. Second, they were not prohibited from having children. In fact, there is an explicit promise that the "seed of woman" would eventually deal a crushing blow to the head of Satan. One of her own would overthrow evil and dispel the darkness of sin (1 John 3:8; Hebrews 2:14).

2. There was no way Eve could grasp the significance of that prophecy. She could grasp that she would have more children (3:16, 20). You have to wonder with the birth of each child, did she think: Is he the one?

3. God's grace was also seen in that He clothed them with "garments of skin"—the first of many blood sacrifices for sin (3:21). He then allowed Eve to conceive and for which she expressed thanks for God's grace (4:1–2). Later she conceived again (4:25) and son, Seth, was born. From Seth would come a line of godly people leading all the way to Christ (Luke 3:38).

When I Get to Heaven,
I'd Like to Tell Eve a Thing or Two

It's easy to be critical of her for ushering in the consequence of sin especially regarding the pain of childbirth. However, we must remember: the only one with the right to be critical is the one who has never likewise sinned (Romans 3:23). Have you ever thought that Eve might be critical of you by asking: Are you as committed to your husband as I was to mine? Or, Have you submitted to my Promised Child as you should—the One who came to this earth and crushed the head of Satan? Makes you think, doesn't it?

Discussion Questions
Prompting Additional Insight

1. What are your initial thoughts when you hear the name "Eve?"

2. Why do you think God doesn't give us a more detailed description of what Eve looked like physically or more specific information about her?

3. Eve was to be a "helper suitable for him" (Genesis 2:18). What does that mean?

4. Picture-paint the scene: Adam awakening from surgery and God's presentation of the woman.
    —From Adam's point of view?
    —From Eve's point of view?

5. Discuss the four foundational pillars of the first marriage (and every marriage to follow) from Genesis 2:24–25:
    —The pillar of *severance*—"a man shall leave his father and his mother"

—The pillar of *permanence*—"and shall cleave to his wife"

—The pillar of *acceptance*—"they shall become one flesh" This includes the sexual union yet encompasses more. It also includes two people growing up and old together and into a lifelong union of "one."

—The pillar of *intimacy*—"and the man and his wife were both naked and were not ashamed."

What happens to the fourth pillar of marriage if the first three are not secure?

6. How could Eve be equal to Adam yet submit lovingly to his leadership in the home? Why do you think the idea of submission meets with such resistance today?

   Follow up: Discuss the command and comparison of both submission (wife) and leadership (husband) as given in Ephesians 5:22–23.

7. As much as anything, it was Eve's craving to be "in the know" that got her into trouble (Genesis 3:4–6). How does Satan tempt us in the same way today?

8. Why did Eve shift the blame when confronted by her sin? Why do we?

9. What life lessons can we learn from both her losses and blessings (banishment from the Garden, loyalty to her husband, promise of future blessing through her seed, pain in childbirth, death of a child, birth of more children, etc.)?

Lesson 3
The Amazing Story of Sarah
Genesis 12–23

By faith even Sarah herself received ability to conceive, even beyond the proper time of life, since she considered Him faithful who had promised.
—Hebrews 11:11—

What a love story—*Abraham and Sarah!* There are some couples whose lives are so bound together that you seldom hear of one without the other. Such was Abraham and Sarah. Even in Hebrews 11, their stories of faith are intertwined. Sarah, the wife of the great patriarch, mother of the promised child (Isaac), example of faith, and the matriarch of Israel—it's easy to paint her character as larger than life. Don't. Scripture doesn't. Like everyone else, she had feet of clay.

Sometimes Sarah is more the example of women behaving badly. We see her at times being manipulative, unreasonable, impatient, angry, jealous, and pouty (not exactly the perfect model of faith and virtue). She was also very attractive—so much so that her husband assumed that even at age sixty-five, she could still turn heads (Genesis 12:11b).

Genesis 11:29 records their marriage. The next verse depicts the fact that would eventually test both her marriage and her faith. "Sarai was barren." She would eventually implement a scheme that would fix that—a scheme that would backfire in her face.

Her faults were obvious and written for all to see. Her faith, however, eventually triumphs. When Peter wrote of a worthy woman for wives to follow, he chose none other than Sarah (1 Peter 3:3–6). And she is the hands-down favorite of the Hebrew writer to stand as the matriarch of Hebrew history (11:11–12). What a study in contrasts! What an *amazing* story . . .

I. Seven Challenges of Faith.

    A. Her upbringing—*The city girl from Ur* . . . Abraham and Sarah came from "Ur of the Chaldeans" (11:31)—near the confluence of the Tigris and Euphrates rivers (modern day Iraq). They literally grew up together (20:12). Here's what else we know:

        • She was Abraham's half sister. Intermarrying would later be forbidden under the Law of Moses.

        • She was ten years younger than Abraham.

        • She and her half-brother/husband were worshipers of Jehovah. As ninth generation descendants of Shem (Noah's son), they represented a remnant of true believers. They would have been contemporaries with Job and Melchizedek.

    God had a plan for the two of them. From them would eventually be born the Messiah who would bless the world (12:3). There was only one problem: "Sarai was barren; she had no child."

    B. Her journey—*Go west young lady* . . . (12:1–3; Hebrews 11:8). To go from their homeland to the River Jordan was no small thing—a journey of 1,000 miles. And they weren't exactly two kids striking out in the twenties (Abraham was seventy-five—12:4). Sarah seems to go willingly. Upon reaching Bethel, they pause long enough for Abraham to construct an altar in recognition of God's promise to give them "this land" (v. 7).

        1. "And Abraham journeyed on . . ." (v. 9). Circumstances did not grow easier, but became increasingly difficult as a famine forced the caravan to Egypt where Abraham feared that Egyptian officials might kill him and kidnap Sarah (vv. 10–12). His solution was to concoct a half-truth lie whereby she would declare herself to be Abraham's sister (v. 13).

        2. Their scheme revealed a flaw in their faith. Abraham was right—the Pharaoh did try to take Sarah into his harem (vv. 14–15) and reward her "brother" lavishly (v. 16). God, however, wasn't pleased and rewarded Pharaoh with

"great plagues" (v. 17). It wasn't long before Egypt's ruler sent them packing back toward the border (12:18—13:3).

C. Her yearning—*An empty crib* . . . What energized Sarah the most were those promises of God—especially the last one (12:3). "Seed" meant one thing: baby. Time passed. No child. Years passed. No child. Sarah wasn't getting any younger, and her biological clock had already expired. What gives?

D. Her foolishness—*Honey, I've got an idea!* Sarah hatched a scheme born of desperation. Although it made perfect sense, it would be one she would regret the rest of her life. In fact, the consequences of her fateful scheme would have far-reaching implications—to this day. The tensions in the Middle East today between Jews and Arabs can be traced to Sarah's foolhardy ploy to concoct a homemade solution to her dilemma.

1. By now Abraham is eighty-five and she seventy-five, post-menopausal and childless (16:3). In her eyes it seemed that God was purposefully withholding children (16:2). He was. But not for the reason she thought. Her plan launched—Abraham could father a child through her much younger Egyptian maid, Hagar. Since Hagar belonged to her, Hagar's offspring would also belong to her. For whatever reason, Abraham doesn't raise any objections (16:2b).

2. God's plan from the beginning was for marriage to be monogamous (Genesis 2:24; Matthew 19:4–5; 1 Corinthians 7:2). Each time that plan is circumvented, disaster follows. This would be no exception.

3. Long story made short: Hagar conceives and pours salt into Sarah's wounds (16:4). In an outburst of jealous anger, Sarah unleashes her scorn at her husband. First, as the leader in his home, Abraham should have consulted the Lord and rejected Sarah's plan. He didn't. Second, Hagar's insolent treatment of Sarah was utterly indefensible. Sadly, Abraham did what many husbands do in times of familial

crisis; he took the path of least resistance by letting Sarah deal with the situation in her own way (16:6).

4. In the midst of this family mess, God showed grace to Hagar and sent her back with a new attitude (vv. 7–9). At the same time, a prophetic word is spoken about her son (vv. 11–12). The final verse in Genesis 16 reveals the age of Abraham (86) at the birth of Ishmael.

E. Her perseverance—*More years of silence* . . . By 17:1 you can add another thirteen years to Abraham's age and the complete loss of hope for Sarah. And yet it is here (17:4) that God speaks of the impossible—again!

1. "And Abraham fell on his face and laughed . . ." (17:17). This is not the laughter of unbelief, but the laughter of belief. By this time Abraham understood that God was fully capable of anything—even the impossible (Romans 4:18–21).

2. In verse 18, the patriarch pleads with God not to overlook Ishmael—a teenager by now. God is plain in His response and in His promise: v. 19. Sarah would conceive and Isaac would be the child of promise. This time the Lord fixes a date: "But My covenant I will establish with Isaac, whom Sarah will bear to you at this season next year" (v. 21).

F. Her joy—*We're going to have a baby!* In Genesis 18, Abraham converses with three angelic guests while Sarah busies herself within earshot (v. 9). The promise is repeated—"Sarah your wife will have a son." She "laughed to herself" at the thought (v. 12). Ninety years old and . . . *pregnant!*

1. In the year that followed, things were busy including (1) the destruction of Sodom, and (2) Abraham up to his old tricks of passing Sarah off as his sister—this time to king Abimelech (same song, second verse). FYI: Sarah was still attractive at age ninety! Regardless, God kicked the king out of bed with this bone-chilling promise: "Behold, you are a dead man because of the woman whom you have taken, for she is married" (20:3). Abimelech

pleaded innocence and sent them on their way.

   2. Finally, in 21:1–3 it happens. Isaac (literally: "laughter") is born. One can only imagine the joy it brought to these two elderly parents.

G. Her harshness—*Get out!* By 21:8, Isaac is a toddler and Ishmael is a teenager. It is then we read: "Now Sarah saw the son of Hagar the Egyptian, whom she had borne to Abraham, mocking . . ." A time of celebration turns into the final straw for Sarah. Too much for her to take, she issues an ultimatum: "Drive out this maid and her son . . ." Although Abraham was distressed (v. 11) it had to be. God would confirm the wisdom of the decision (vv. 12–21).

   1. Yet even in the time of harshness for Hagar and Ishmael, God watched over them (v. 20).

   2. Even though the boys grew up apart, they would maintain a familial relationship through their father. Oddly enough, when Abraham died, both boys came together once more to give their father a proper burial (25:8–9).

II. Watching Isaac Grow.

A. The separation scene of toddler Isaac and teenager Ishmael is the last we read of Sarah until she dies. Genesis 23:1–2 records her death and the mourning of Abraham over his sweet Sarah.

B. It was a love story from beginning to end. Indeed, if Abraham was the father of the faithful, Sarah was the matriarch of all who would follow in their steps. As Scripture is clear to point out, she was anything but perfect. She was, however, one amazing woman.

Discussion Questions
Prompting Additional Insight

1. What is your first impression of Sarah?

2. Hebrews 11:8–10 presents the faith of Abraham—trusting God enough to pull up tent stakes and strike out "not knowing where he was going." What does that also say about Sarah?

3. How does Abraham describe her at age sixty-five (12:11b)? I've never met a woman yet who isn't encouraged by compliments from a husband who notices.

4. Abraham noticed. Would you agree that spouses need to do a better job "noticing" one another and the positive traits that brought them together in the first place? Why do we stop "noticing" and how can we work to re-start?

   Follow up: What would be your counsel toward one who is struggling because her husband no longer notices and compliments?

5. Obviously Sarah was attractive and, rather than letting herself go, she worked to enhance her beauty both outward and inward. In fact, she is mentioned in 1 Peter 3:1–6 as an example of such. As a woman of God, how do you find the balance between outer beauty and having an inside heart for the Lord?

6. She had her flaws. For example, she does not question her husband about deceiving the Egyptians about her marital status (seeking to protect him). Instead, what should she have encouraged her husband to do?

7. "Wait upon the Lord" is difficult to do when the Lord's timing is not ours. Sarah was promised a child. By 16:1–2 and seventy-five years of age, it was obvious (at least to her) that it was not going to happen. Discuss:
    —Her disastrous Plan B
    —The rift it caused in the family
    —Abraham's failure of leadership

8. What was Abraham's response to the Lord's promise when he turned the Big 100? (17:17)? What was Sarah's response (18:12)? What would have been your response?

9. What tender picture of the aged Abraham is painted for us in 23:1–2? Abraham and Sarah—an amazing story of two becoming one and growing in their faith.

Lesson 4

The Amazing Story of Jochebed

Exodus 2:1–10

*But when she could hide him no longer, she got him a wicker basket
and covered it over with tar and pitch. Then she put the child into it
and set it among the reeds by the bank of the Nile.*
—Exodus 2:3—

How many important people have risen from difficult backgrounds—the ghettos of life—and who, in spite of the obstacles in front of them and the odds stacked against them, overcame the hardships to make significant contributions to society? The answer: a bunch.

Political leaders, entertainers, athletes—the list is endless. And the same is true of personages found in Scripture. Not everyone in the Bible was born of nobility or into a family of wealth.

- Jephthah's birth was illegitimate and his mother a prostitute. Shunned by his siblings, he ran away from home where he raised himself on the streets of Judah. By the remarkable grace of God, Jephthah overcame and went on to become one of the judges of Israel (Judges 11:1—12:7).
- Hadasseh was an orphan being raised by her cousin. Scripture says "she had no father or mother." However, she went on to become the Queen of Persia and eventually would save the Jews from annihilation. You probably know her by her Persian name: Esther.
- Onesimus was a runaway slave who became a Christian. When Paul wrote a postcard to his owner (Philemon), the apostle said, "He was useless to you, but now is useful both to you and to me" (v. 11). Another great to arise from the ghetto . . .

And now one more. The story behind the baby in the basket, hidden among the reeds of the Nile, is the faith of his mother: a woman named *Jochebed*—an ingenious and amazing woman.

I.   The Ghetto of Goshen, Exodus 1–2.
    A.   Affliction and oppression . . . The descendants of Joseph settled in an area of Egypt called "Goshen" (Genesis 47:1, 27). By the time of Exodus 1, they had multiplied greatly and became servants to a new Pharaoh who "did not know Joseph" (Exodus 1:6–8). Thousands of Hebrews were forced into hard labor to eke out an existence under the heavy hand of the Egyptian king.
        1.   Feeling threatened by their numbers, (vv. 9–10), Pharaoh sought to solve the problem through strict oversight and control (v. 11). When that didn't work (because God was at work), he increased their labor (vv. 12–14).
        2.   It's hard to imagine what they faced. As the Egyptians turned up the demands and control, the land of Goshen became a hopeless and horrible ghetto of slavery. Perhaps the only thing to which Hebrew families could look forward was the birth of a baby. Before long, however, even that glimmer of hope was extinguished (vv. 15–16).
    B.   Murder and midwives . . . It's emotional enough to go through the rigors of a nine month pregnancy only to give birth and hear the words: *"It's a boy!"*—knowing that you would never see your baby again. The Hebrew midwives, however, "feared God" above man and "did not do as the king of Egypt commanded them, but let the boys live" (v. 17).
        1.   When Pharaoh saw that the midwives would not cooperate with his plan, he issued an edict enlisting the cooperation of all Egyptian citizens: "Every son [Jewish boy] who is born you are to cast into the Nile . . ." (v. 22).
        2.   It's not hard to imagine the household searches and the horror of holocaust that swept through every Hebrew

home. By the way, Pharaoh was not the last to attempt horrible atrocities against the Jews.

II. Two Parents: Amram and Jochebed.
  A. Their faith, 2:1–2 (we learn their names in 6:20). They already had two children: Aaron, age three (7:7) and Miriam (probably a teenager—2:4; Numbers 26:59). Hebrews 11:23 gives special mention of their faith: "By faith Moses, when he was born, was hidden for three months by his parents, because they saw he was a beautiful child; and they were not afraid of the king's edict."
    1. The faith of Amram and Jochebed caused them to do everything within their power to save the life of their baby. Their prayer was undoubtedly that of Psalm 91:1–2—a prayer of trust in the refuge of God.
    2. They would not be intimidated by the most powerful man on earth. They would protect their baby at the cost of their own lives.
  B. Their creativity. "When she could hide him no longer . . ." One writer paints a vivid and emotional picture . . .

Finally the mother was led by God to weave papyri rushes into a little ark; covering it with tar to make it impervious to wet. And there she put the little child with many a kiss. She closed the lid upon his sweet face and with her own hand, bore it to the water's edge and placed it tenderly among the flags that grew there.

She knew that Pharaoh's daughter came there to bathe and it might be that she would see the little foundling and rescue him—and if not, then the God who she trusted would help her in some other way.

Jochebed went home fighting a mother's natural anxiety by a faith which had clasped the arm of the living God who could not fail her.

1. That's faith! Later, how can we be surprised at the faith of Moses seeing that he was born into such a faith-nurturing home?

2. The plan was ingenious (vv. 4–6). You can imagine the rehearsal between mother and Miriam: When Pharaoh's daughter sees him, immediately step up and ask if she would like one of the Hebrew women to nurse him . . . And that's what happened (vv. 7–9). With the blessing of Pharaoh's daughter, Jochebed became the paid nurse and nanny for her own son. That's creativity. That's faith. That's God at work.

III. Concentrated Nurturing.

A. Knowing that she would only have a few years, Jochebed would make each moment count. Verse 10—The child grew and she brought him to Pharaoh's daughter and he became her son. And she named him Moses, and said, "Because I drew him out of the water."

1. Are you telling me that the few years Moses was under the influence of his mother, made a difference? Read Hebrews 11:24–26. Why did Moses walk away? And where did he learn that? The "by faith he left Egypt not fearing the wrath of the king . . ." (v. 27) sounds strikingly similar to the "by faith Moses, when he was born, was hidden . . . because his parents were not afraid of the king" either (v. 23). Where else do you think Moses learned to have such faith and trust in God?

2. Life was rugged in Jochebed's world of slavery. In the little time she had, she gave her young son all she had. Not a moment could be wasted. Call it what it was: concentrated nurturing.

B. Her time was short, but so is yours. And even if you are given eighteen years, it's still short. If you don't believe that, ask a mom who just watched her son leave for college or go off into the service. Suddenly eighteen years seem like the blur that it is.

1. Don't waste a single day. Don't waste a single opportunity to teach and train your children that the same God who watched over Moses, will watch over them. By the way mom, He will watch over you, too.
2. Isn't that the between-the-lines message of Deuteronomy 6:5–9?

IV. Two Timeless Truths:

A. It's possible to *over*-state the impact of a child's environment. As difficult and as threatening an environment as Goshen became, God overruled.

1. Yes, with His help you can raise good kids in an evil world. Don't be a fatalist. Jochebed wasn't. She wrapped her arms around the living God and trusted in Him. She trusted Him when she placed the little basket into the Nile and . . . a few years later she trusted again when she placed her young son into the hands of Pharaoh's daughter—and watched as her boy walked into the palace.
2. Jochebed knew he would be raised there, but she knew he wouldn't stay there. Her son was not an Egyptian; he was an Israelite. And she poured that knowledge (and faith!) into him every single day.

Not for the star-crowned heroes, the men who conquer and slay,
But a song for those who bore them; the mothers braver they.
With never a blare of trumpets, with never a surge of cheers,
They marched to the unseen hazards—pale, patient, volunteers.
—Anonymous—

B. It's possible to *under*-state the importance of parenting.

1. That's motherhood. If Jochebed could whisper in your ear, she would say, It's worth it all! All the anxious moments

... All the sleepless nights ... All the hours of crying and counsel ...

2. God isn't looking for perfect moms raising up brilliant kids. He just wants you to be there for them, be available to them, and maximize every moment you have to build their faith.

3. Sadly, so few take it seriously. Harassed by media and culture, motherhood is cut down to the level of second-rate slavery. It isn't. It is the most important role in the world. Jochebed's message is clear: It's worth it all. And who knows, you may even have a Moses on your hands!

In a time of trouble, in a time forlorn,
  There's a hiding place where hope is born.
In a time of danger when our faith is proved,
  There's a hiding place where we are loved.

There's a hiding place—a strong protected space
  Where God provides the grace to persevere.
For nothing can remove us from the Father's love,
  Though all may change, nothing changes here.

In a time of sorrow, in time of grief,
  There's a hiding place to give relief.
In a time of weakness, in a time of fear,
  There's a hiding place where God is near.
                                    —Brian Jeffery Leach

Discussion Questions
Prompting Additional Insight

1. Discuss the growing hardships faced by the Hebrews in Exodus 1:8–22.

2. What did Pharaoh instruct the Hebrew midwives to do to the male babies? What did they do? Why?

3. How do you think Jochebed was able to walk away from the water's edge knowing her baby was there?

4. Read Exodus 2:5–9. Coincidence or providence?

5. Perhaps you know single moms or those facing dire financial situations where they must leave their children and go into the workforce to provide the necessities of life. What do you think would be Jochebed's message to them?

6. How important is a mother's influence on a child during those formative years?

7. What principles of parenting are found in Deuteronomy 6:4–9? Who wrote Deuteronomy? How would Moses know the truth of these verses?

8. Discuss ways parents can overcome difficult environments to raise up godly kids.

Lesson 5

The Amazing Story of Rahab
Joshua 2

By faith Rahab the harlot did not perish along with those who were
disobedient, after she had welcomed the spies in peace.
—Hebrews 11:31—

Rahab the harlot. There's no hiding who she was or what she had done. That simple two-word tag-line follows her throughout Scripture. Open her closet and the skeletons are there for all to see.

When she is first introduced, Rahab is one of the most unsavory of characters (Joshua 2:1). Chances are, if you had met her before the turning point in her life, you would have written her off as hopeless. She certainly would not have been high on anyone's personal prospect list for conversion to the God of Israel. She was an immoral woman living in the midst of a pagan culture fanatically devoted to everything God hates.

Jericho was a town of the Amorites who, because of their wickedness, would fall to the Joshua-led army of Israel. Only by the grace of God and the actions her faith, was she saved from destruction.

Not only did Rahab come to know the God of the Israelites, she became a role model of faith. In fact, of the noteworthy's of the Old Testament who played a role in God's plan for man's redemption, Rahab is one of two women (Sarah) singled out in Hebrews 11. And James adds (2:25): "In the same way, was not Rahab the harlot also justified by works when she received the messengers and sent them out by another way?" And get this: her name even appears in the genealogy of Jesus (Matthew 1:5–6).

The story of Rahab reminds us that these women were not footnotes to God's plan, but were at the very heart of it. Their stories are absolutely amazing. And Rahab's story is no exception.

I. An Unlikely Heroine.
    A. Rahab was not only a citizen of Jericho, but her house was located—not on some back alley—but perched strategically on the famous wall itself (Joshua 2:15). In modern-day vernacular, we would say she lived in a "high traffic" area which undoubtedly gave her "business" good visibility. I doubt it's a stretch to say that most citizens of Jericho knew where she lived. The Bible doesn't airbrush what she did. She was a prostitute.

History 101

1. Moses had died—along with the generation that came out of Egypt.
2. There were two exceptions: Joshua and Caleb.
3. Under Joshua's leadership, the nation of Israel was poised to invade the Promised Land.
4. Joshua sent spies secretly across the Jordan with the instructions: "Go view the land, especially Jericho (2:1)." It was a reconnaissance mission in preparation for the coming invasion.

    B. When the spies came to Jericho "they came to Rahab's house" (2:1b). Little did she know that these two Jewish strangers would change her life. By God's providence, a woman whose life was dependent upon evil would find grace.

II. An Unexpected Act of Kindness (Joshua 2:2–7).
    A. From the Israelite encampment to the Jordan River required an approximate seven mile walk. The spies must ford the river then walk an additional seven miles to the city. Scripture doesn't mention how they gained entrance. Jericho was a large city on a successful trade route and travelers came and

went continually. Perhaps they mingled in among others. Once inside, it was essential they avoid suspicion. They quite possibly were drawn to Rahab's house for two reasons:

1. Her house was on the wall (literally)—a perfect location from which to spy and secure a means of escape if necessary.

2. Because of her "profession," Rahab would have opened the door to strangers without asking too many questions. She was, after all, in the business of confidentiality.

B. The Israelite men did not seek her out for immoral purposes (which may have been the thing that won her trust), but treated her respectfully. By God's providence, they had come to the right place and found the right person. Unknown to them, Rahab's heart was ready to learn more about Jehovah (vv. 9–11).

1. The fact that Joshua's army was encamped nearby was no secret. And what Israel's God had done for them was no secret either. All of which meant one thing: the city was on heightened alert.

2. Someone had, in fact, seen them and reported their presence to the authorities (v. 2)—perhaps following them to Rahab's dwelling (v. 3). When questioned, Rahab misdirected the officials and saved the lives of the two Israelites. Verse 6 reveals her quick thinking—"But she had brought them up to the roof and hidden them in the stalks of flax which she had laid in order on the roof."

C. "The" question . . . Was Rahab justified in lying? It is a question that has confounded many. The answer is simple. The answer is . . . no.

1. The Bible is clear about lying (Exodus 20:16; Proverbs 12:22; Colossians 3:9). Some argue that "all is fair in love and war," but such a situational approach to ethics is fraught with difficulties.

2. I see no reason to justify Rahab's lie. Was it necessary for the greater good? No. God's plan would not have been

halted if she had remained silent. He would have found another way to protect those men or allowed them to escape. The three Hebrew boys in Daniel could have escaped by lying, too. They didn't. The same could be said for first century Christians.

3. There is no need to justify her lie, and Scripture never does (any more than it justifies her former profession). Rahab is not applauded for her ethics; she is applauded for her faith and the fact that she acted upon it. In time, she would learn—a lot. For the moment, she embraced these men and staked her life on what she had heard about the God of Israel.

III. Faith, Fear, and a Future.

A. Perhaps this is not the first time Rahab had hidden someone. Apparently the stalks of flax ("which she had laid on the roof," v. 6) were there for this very reason—should a jealous wife come looking for her husband. Is it also coincidental that she had a rope handy (v. 15) that was long enough to allow them to escape over the wall?

1. Note the biblical account: vv. 8–14. Her faith was motivated by fear. She had heard about Jehovah's strength and knew He was capable of destroying the city.

2. The spies' promise of protection was conditional upon one thing—vv. 17–18. The scarlet cord that had facilitated their escape would also be the sign of her escape. If she followed their instructions, Rahab and her house would be spared the coming destruction. On the other hand . . . v. 20.

B. The spies descended under the cover of darkness by means of her scarlet rope and hid secretly in the hills for three days until the Jericho patrols subsided. They then crossed over the Jordan and made their way back to Joshua and the Israelite encampment where they brought positive news (based in large part upon intelligence gathered from Rahab) that the city was ripe for conquering (vv. 21–24).

IV. Her Legacy.
   A. Joshua 6 . . . God would orchestrate the invasion of Jericho in such a way that would leave no doubt that He was fighting alongside Israel. He would demolish those massive Jericho walls without any military muscle at all. And the walls came tumbling down . . . (v. 20).
      1. When the walls of Jericho fell flat, there was one amazing exception: "the harlot's house" (vv. 22–23). Verse 25— "However, Rahab the harlot and her father's household and all she had, Joshua spared . . ." (v. 25a). Joshua (compiling Israel's history some time later) added a simple post script: "and she has lived in the midst of Israel to this day, for she hid the messengers whom Joshua sent to spy out Jericho" (v. 25b).
      2. Oddly enough, after the conquest of Jericho, Rahab is never mentioned again in the Old Testament. When she resurfaces on the pages of Scripture it is in the New Testament. She appears in Hebrews 11 as a member of the hall of history's faithful, and in James in a discussion of the importance of having a faith that works.
   B. The most amazing part of her legacy is that she appears in the opening lines of Matthew's genealogy of Jesus. Matthew traces Jesus' ancestors back to Abraham—and there she is . . . Rahab—Boaz—Obed—Jesse—David . . .
      1. Perhaps Rahab is there to remind us that God's grace cleanses the worst of sinners. As Jesus stated clearly—"It is not those who are healthy who need a physician, but those who are sick" (Matthew 9:12).
      2. Some Jewish scholars have been embarrassed by Rahab and merely describe her as an "innkeeper." No, the Greek word translated harlot is *porne* from which we get such words as pornography. There is no need to sanitize

her background. As one writer said, "Remove the stigma of sin and you remove the need for grace." She was what she was. It makes her story all the more amazing—not because of what she was, but because of what she became because of her faith. That is the lesson of Rahab's life. And ours, too.

Discussion Questions
Prompting Additional Insight

1. Why do you think Scripture reminds us of Rahab's past each time she is mentioned?

2. Compare Hebrews 11:31 with James 2:25. In the first passage, Rahab is saved by her faith; in the second, she is justified by her works. What is the point of both verses about faith and works— and how does it relate to us?

3. The fact that the two spies came to Rahab's house was more than coincidence—it was providence. Providence has been defined as God working behind the scenes without interrupting the on- going of human affairs. While we do not understand how God works His providence nor understand His timing, we can see it in such stories as Rahab. In view of verses like Matthew 7:7-8, do you think God's providence continues to work today? Have you seen evidence of it in your own life?

4. Rahab saved the spies at considerable risk to herself. If the truth had been discovered, she might have been killed. If she turned them over to the authorities, she might have been rewarded. What caused her to protect them?

5. Nowhere does Scripture condone lying—and it doesn't in Rahab's case (any more than it condones her immoral life). In time, Rahab would learn to trust God to the point that lying would not be necessary. The Bible and history is filled with examples of godly people who told the truth—at times costing them their lives. How strong was the faith of the three Hebrew boys in Daniel 3? What was their declaration to the king in vv. 17–18? What is the lesson for us?

6. How does the declaration of Zechariah 4:6 sum up the battle of Jericho?

7. The wall of Jericho fell down flat . . ." (Joshua 6:20). What strange sign would save Rahab's house?

8. Undoubtedly, Rahab turned her back on her past and changed the course of her future. When Joshua penned the memoirs of Israel (6:25), where was Rahab?

9. The lesson of Rahab isn't what she had been, but what she would become. There are people serving Christ today who you would have never thought would change and come to Him. What is the modern message for us in the Rahab story?

Lesson 6

The Amazing Story of Ruth
The Book of Ruth

"Your people shall be my people, and your God, my God."
—Ruth 1:16—

It is the Harlequin romance story of Scripture. Even though it is told in short-story format (eighty-five verses), it runs the full gamut of human emotions—from gut-wrenching grief to the heights of happiness. It is one of the most heart-warming stories you will ever read.

Ruth, a young widow and foreigner, faced a decision. Bereft of her husband yet dedicated to her mother-in-law (Naomi), this young Moabite woman was poised to learn about the God of Israel. Like the story of Rahab, you can't fail to see the providence of God working behind the scenes. And like Rahab, Ruth finds her way into the genealogy of Jesus (Matthew 1:5).

We are reminded again that the story of Scripture is the story of the fulfillment of the three promises to Abraham in Genesis 12:1–3.

1. The land promise—to Abraham's descendants would be given the land of Canaan—fulfilled in Joshua 21:43.
2. The nation promise—that from Abraham would arise a great nation—fulfilled post-exodus in the giving of the Law of Moses to govern God's Old Testament people.
3. The seed promise—that one would arise from Abraham who would bless all mankind. That "one" would be Jesus (Galatians 3:16).

Thus the story of the Old Testament is the story of the people of Abraham living in the land promised to Abraham waiting for the coming Messiah. The book of Ruth gives us a brief, snap-shot insight into the lives of some descendants of Abraham and ancestors of Jesus: focusing on an unlikely widow who happened—coincidence or providence?—to give birth to the great-grandfather of David. It's what makes this story so *amazing!*

I. A Story of Life and Loss.
    A. Family and famine, 1:1–2. "Now it came about in the days when the judges governed . . ." This was near the end of the era of the judges (one hundred years before David). The book of Judges reports that during this time God's people went through periods of rebellion. God would punish them in different ways—even using natural calamities such as a famine (v. 1).
        1. Elimelech and his wife, Naomi, were from Bethlehem (the burial place of Rachel and future hometown of David). Little did they know they would become a key link in the chain of the messianic line. Their hometown would play a role; they would play a role.
        2. The famine forced Elimelech to relocate his family. Looking for food and opportunity, they moved to Moab. FYI: The Moabites were descendants of Lot, Abraham's nephew. More specifically, Lot's oldest daughter had a child via an incestuous relationship with her father. The child born from that illicit union was named: "Moab" (Genesis 19:37). Although the Israelites and Moabites shared a common ancestor, they despised each other.
        3. The Moabites became idolatrous and represented everything that God abhorred. Thus it is somewhat shocking that Elimelech would take his family there. Desperate times, however, call for desperate decisions. Perhaps he felt as if he had little choice.
    B. Trial and tragedy. Times went from bad to worse (v. 3) with the loss of the bread-winner. Even though the Israelites were forbidden to intermarry with the Canaanites

(Deuteronomy 7), her sons, Mahlon and Chilion, took Moabites wives—Orpah and Ruth. Perhaps feeling trapped by hardship, they married women who seemed teachable. Regardless, they remained there for the next decade (v. 4).

1. Then more tragedy struck, v. 5. Scripture does not give the details, but suffice it to say, Naomi is heartbroken. She is now widowed, childless, impoverished, aging, and in a foreign land. She longed to go home (v. 6).

2. Yet such a move was not without consequences. She would leave behind the burial site for both her husband and her sons. She would also leave behind her daughters-in-law.

3. At first, it appeared that all three would make the journey to Bethlehem (v. 7). At some point Naomi stopped. Was she really being fair to them? She gathered her strength and made an impassioned plea for them to remain in their own land. Verses 8–14 is heart-wrenching to read.

II. Ruth's Life-Changing Decision.

A. Orpah returns (v. 14). Ruth hesitates (v. 15). Did Naomi really believe it was better for Ruth to return to "her gods?" Perhaps it was a test of Ruth's faith. Undoubtedly, Naomi had taught her daughters-in-law about the one true God of Israel. In a moment of decision, how committed would they be?

1. It is here that Ruth speaks words for which she will always be remembered (vv. 16–17). She would remain with Naomi and journey back to Judah. Her devotion to Naomi and to the God of Naomi was real (v. 18). Such is impressive when you understand the pagan culture in which she was raised.

2. Naomi's arrival back in Bethlehem caused no small stir (vv. 19–20). "Do not call me "Naomi; call me Mara" [bitter]. It wasn't that Naomi had become a bitter person, but that she had endured a life of bitter grief. Perhaps she

sensed the Lord was testing her (like Job). Although she didn't understand, she didn't give up (v. 21).
3. Finally, after a decade away, Naomi was home (v. 22).

Ruth 2:1 is parenthetical. It is here we are introduced to a Bethlehem relative: Boaz. He was a direct descendant of Rahab (Matt.1:5). Boaz would have a natural sympathy toward a foreigner in Israel—a woman who had embraced faith in God as had his own mother.

III. Ruth's Redemption.
A. The younger Ruth would have to support the aging Naomi. The Law protected the poor by stating that they could earn their food by gleaning the leftovers from the field (Leviticus 19:9–10). In Israel, if you were willing to work, God made a way for you to eat. Ruth was willing to work (v. 2).
   1. "And she happened to come to the field belonging to Boaz" (v. 3). *Question:* coincidence or providence? When Boaz happened along, Ruth caught his eye and he made inquiry (v. 5). Finding out that she was a relative (v. 6), he granted her protection and special favors (vv. 8–9).
   2. Ruth is taken aback by his kindness (v. 10). Boaz reveals that he is aware of the sacrifice she had already made for Naomi (vv. 11–12).
   3. It's not hard to read between the lines and see that there is something else happening (vv. 14-16). Verse 17 states that she gleaned "an ephah of barley" (half a bushel—which is a lot for someone gathering leftovers).
   4. When Ruth told her mother-in-law about Boaz, Naomi recognized the hand of God (v. 20). Her wheels began to turn (vv. 20–23). It was customary in Judah for the nearest male relative to step forward and assume the family duties. It looked to Naomi as if Boaz was thinking along those same lines.
B. This was a culture of "arranged marriages." It was also customary for the man in the house to arrange the marriages.

In this case, there was no man in the house. Thus, Naomi stepped in to work a little match-making-magic and hurry things along.

1. Chapter 3 begins with Naomi giving counsel to Ruth. Now here is what you need to do . . .

2. There is nothing immoral about her advice (vv. 2–4). Wait until he is asleep, then lie down at his feet . . . Oddly enough, it was a way for Ruth to propose marriage (they did things a lot different back then). Ruth followed Naomi's advice (vv. 5–9). Verse 9 is literally, "Spread your covering over your maid, for you are my redeemer."

3. Boaz understood, acknowledged her proposal, and spoke of her reputation in the city (vv. 7–11).

C. There was one problem. Boaz was aware of a male relative closer in kinship than he (vv. 12–13). Jewish custom stated that Boaz must defer to him. Disappointed and somewhat anxious, Ruth left early the next morning (v. 14). Boaz, however, doesn't let her get away empty-handed (v. 15).

1. Naomi is waiting for word from Ruth (v. 16). She brings her mother-in-law the report—and "six measures of barley." Even the fact that Boaz had some unfinished "family business" to see after did not take away her smile. She recognized the providential hand of God at work (v. 18).

2. "Now Boaz went up to the gate . . ." and confronted the male relative with an offer (4:1–4). The law stated that if a family had to sell land to pay their debts, they must be allowed to buy it back at a later time. The male relative agreed to the transaction.

3. That's when Boaz threw him a curve. "On the day you buy the field from the hand of Naomi, you must also acquire Ruth the Moabitess, the widow of the deceased, in order to raise up the name of the deceased on his inheritance" (v. 5). Long story short: you buy the land, you marry Ruth! Suddenly the unnamed relative had second thoughts

and decided to pass (v. 6). He forfeited his right to the next of kin—Boaz!

4. The agreement was blessed by the city elders (vv. 9–12). Boaz was now free and clear to marry Ruth. And he wasted little time (v. 13). Soon thereafter, God blessed Boaz and Ruth with a baby boy they named "Obed" (v. 17)—the pride and joy of his grandmother (vv. 14–16).

Ruth—Obed—Jesse—David . . . Jesus!

The grieving Moabite widow would become the great-grandmother of King David and thus join the lineage of Jesus. What an amazing story!

Discussion Questions
Prompting Additional Insight

1. What is the historical time setting according to Ruth 1:1? Describe the ups and downs of that time period.

2. In the depths of grief . . . Describe Naomi's grief in chapter one: (1) her husband dies—v. 3, (2) her sons marry Moabite women—v. 4, (3) her sons die, v. 5. What life-changing decision did she make?

3. What advice would you give someone who is contemplating marriage to a man who isn't a Christian?

4. At first all three women began to travel to Judah (1:7). What do you think motivated Naomi to encourage her daughters-in-law to remain in Moab?

5. How strong was Ruth's pledge of loyalty to Naomi? What between-the-lines insight does this give you about Naomi, her faith, and her influence upon Ruth?

6. One source of potential marital strife can be in-law difficulties. What counsel would you give mothers about respecting the boundaries of a new home?

    Follow-up—Sometimes it's not the mother-in-law who is the problem. How can daughters-in-law work to make for a better relationship? And how can the mothers of daughters work to train them to appreciate the mother of the man they married?

7. What had Boaz heard about Ruth (2:11–12)? How did that have a familiar ring, given the story of his own mother?

8. What was Naomi's plan for hurrying Boaz along?

9. Long story made short . . . Boaz and Ruth married and "the Lord enabled her to conceive, and she gave birth to a son. Then the women said to Naomi, 'Blessed is the Lord who has not left you without a redeemer today, and may his name become famous in Israel,'" (4:13–14). Did his name become "famous in Israel"?

10. About Boaz, Naomi said, "He is one of our closest relatives," (2:20b). The Hebrew word means "redeemer; one who rescues." In what sense are we redeemed and exalted to be our Redeemer's bride?

The Amazing Story of Hannah
1 Samuel 1–2

*She made a vow and said, "O Lord of hosts, if you will indeed look on
the affliction of Your maidservant and remember me . . . but will give
your maidservant a son, then I will give him to the Lord
all the days of his life . . ."*
—1 Samuel 1:11—

Hannah Grace—It's one of the most popular biblical names for girls—and good reason. If any woman of Scripture stands as an example of grace and godliness, it is Hannah. In fact, her name means "grace." How fitting.

Like Sarah, Hannah thought she would never hear the cry of a baby—her baby. Both women were childless and distraught. Both were plagued by stress brought on by their husband's bigamy. Both received the blessing from the Lord they so desperately sought. Sarah's son would become one of the patriarchs of Israel. Hannah's son would be the last of the judges and live to anoint the royal line of the Messiah through David. They had much in common as both of them overcame hardship to become examples of faith.

Hannah was also a lot like Mary:
- Both offered prayers of exultation (1 Samuel 2:1–10; Luke 1:46–55) expressing praise for the holiness of God.
- Both dedicated their "firstborn" to the Lord.
- Both were bereaved due to physical separation because of sons who embarked on spiritual missions.

While Scripture focuses more on their firstborn sons, our study will focus on the mothers who bore them.

The story of Hannah is indeed a story of feminine grace and faith. Her appearance on the pages of Scripture, albeit brief, is nonetheless *amazing*.

I. Samuel's Godly Heritage.
    A. She was an obscure women living in a remote part of Israel. 1 Samuel 1:1-2 introduces us to Hannah and her husband, Elkanah (who happened to be the great, great grandfather of Zuph—which has no real significance except that . . . it's a non-used Bible name still up for grabs).
        1. Elkanah is described as an "Ephraimite," but only because he lived there. By tribe he was really a Levite (1 Chronicles 6:27–28) and the Levites had no territory of their own. Look at any map of the tribes of Israel and there is no territory known as "Levi." The Levites were the priestly tribe and, as such, were scattered throughout Israel.
        2. Thus Elkanah the Levite is called an "Ephraimite" because he lived in Ephraim. As a priest, however, Elkanah would take his turn each year serving in the tabernacle at Shiloh (v. 3)—which was also located in Ephraim. Here's what we have so far:
            a. Elkanah and Hannah lived in the hill country of Ephraim.
            b. Periodically they would travel the fifteen miles from their home in Ramah to worship at the tabernacle in Shiloh.
        3. That's important because some have the mistaken idea that Hannah would later "drop off" Samuel in Shiloh and never see him again. That's not exactly the case.
    B. These were dismal days in Israel's history—for three reasons:
        1. Two of the worst priests in history were serving in Shiloh (v. 3b). The sons of Eli were notoriously wicked—and everyone knew it (2:12, 22).

2. The Ark of the Covenant (previously located in Shiloh) was gone. It had been captured and carried off by the Philistines.

3. Word from God was rare in those days (3:1b). The Israelites were adrift without leadership. They needed someone who could turn their hearts back to God. That someone would be . . . Samuel. And the hand that rocked his cradle would be . . . Hannah.

II. Holy Ambition.

   A. Hannah's home-life was troubled. "He [Elkanah] had two wives: the name of the one was Hannah and the name of the other Peninnah" (1:2). It appears that Elkanah had married Hannah first (since her name appears first). Later, he probably married Peninnah in order to bear children and continue the family name. Elkanah loved Hannah deeply (vv. 4–5) and Peninnah knew it. Jealous for the love of her husband, Peninnah would "provoke her [Hannah] bitterly to irritate her" (vv. 6–7). It grieved Hannah to the point that she "wept and would not eat."

III. The Three Great Loves of Hannah's Life.

   A. She loved her husband, v. 5. The love between Elkanah and Hannah seemed mutual. If Hannah had been able to bear children, Elkanah would not have married wife number two. But he did—and the polygamy fallout was predictable (it always is).

      1. The key to family life doesn't center on children—it centers on the commitment that a man and a woman make in marriage (Genesis 2:24). Yes, children are a blessing of the Lord (Psalm 127:3–4), but they must never be the glue that holds a marriage into place. If so, what happens to the marriage when the children are grown and gone?

    2.   Elkanah and Hannah traveled together to worship at Shiloh (v. 3a, 7a, 9a, 19a).

B. She loved her God. It is obvious from her prayer that Hannah was a woman of deep passion for the Lord (vv. 9–11). This was no selfish prayer as if to "show up" her rival. Her petition was entirely self-less. She did not ask for many children, only one.

    1.   "Now it came about as she continued praying before the Lord" (v. 12a). This was no quick burst of prayer. She stayed and continued to pray fervently.

    2.   Hannah made two vows before God: (1) "I will give him to the Lord . . . " This was more than promising to raise up a son to be a godly young man. She was promising him for full time service at the tabernacle in Shiloh. (2) "And a razor shall never come on his head." A Nazarite vow represented a sign of spiritual devotion (e.g. Samson, John the Baptist).

    3.   Hannah prayed so intently that she caught the eye of Eli, the high priest (vv. 12–14). Obviously Eli wasn't used to seeing people pray with much emotion. Perhaps had he done more of the same himself, his own boys may have turned out differently. Or maybe he thought she was one of the "loose ladies" with whom his sons liked to consort. Regardless, his first impression was not accurate and his rebuke was rude.

    4.   Hannah answered the high priest with grace and humility (vv. 15–16). Eli quickly changed his tune and, in turn, pronounced a blessing on her (vv. 17–18).

    5.   We aren't surprised at what happened next. The Lord took heed to her prayer, blessed her, and "she gave birth to a son." She named him "Samuel" (vv. 19–20).

C. She loved her home. Samuel was a living answer to prayer and a daily reminder of God's grace. Hannah was as devoted to her son as any first-time mom would be. When the time came for Elkanah to travel back to Shiloh, mother and child stayed behind (vv. 21–22). The time would come—and sooner than she wished— but not yet. These were the precious days of childhood memories, and she was determined to make each one count.

1. Hannah was the quintessential stay-at-home-mom. She was the fixture in his formative years. It is said that most of a child's personality is formed in the first few years. Hannah would be there to shape, mold, and teach young Samuel about the God who had blessed her with him.

2. She knew what was coming. The day arrived when she must pack his things and take him to Shiloh (vv. 24–25). We aren't sure his exact age although Scripture says "the child was young" (v. 24). How could she trust her young son into the care of Eli and his worthless sons? She didn't. She trusted him into the hands of the One who had answered her prayer. And if God had answered that prayer, He would answer this one (vv. 26–28).

3. "Then Elkanah went to his home at Ramah. But the boy ministered to the Lord before Eli the priest" (2:11). It was a long ride home.

IV. Final Thoughts.

A. Don't you know she counted the days between visits (2:18–19). Each year she would make him a new robe—and a bigger one. Eli was glad to have Samuel and used him. The scene of Elkanah and Hannah coming to Shiloh became a welcome one for the high priest. On one such trip, he blessed them again (vv. 20–21). Same story second verse. And then third verse. And then fourth verse. And then *fifth* verse (v. 21). Her home and family had become rich and full. Her love for God, Elkanah, and Samuel remained a priority the rest of her days.

B. Those were dark days. One man changed all that—Samuel. He grew up and became a man—God's man—a prophet and the last judge in Israel. He would anoint the first king (Saul) and later anoint David. Two Old Testament books are named after him. Centuries later, both Peter and Paul would mention him in their sermons. He is listed in hall of the faithful (Heb.11). As his life neared the end, he would spend his remaining days back at the old home place in Ramah— (1 Samuel 25:1)—forever thankful for a mother who loved him enough that she selflessly raised him to serve the Lord. Samuel's influence upon Israel cannot be overstated. Then, again, the same can be said for the influence of his mother upon him. It is one amazing story.

Discussion Questions
Prompting Additional Insight

1. Read the prayer of Hannah in 1 Samuel 2:1–10. This is no half-hearted prayer of a bitter woman who made a rash vow and regretted it the rest of her life. Instead, it gives you insight into Hannah's soul. What do you see?

2. It's hard for us to understand ancient cultural pressures for a man to have children to carry on the family name. With a barren wife, what decision did Elkanah make? In what ways did it grieve the heart of Hannah?

3. Elkanah didn't get it (1:8). "Hannah, why do you weep and why do you not eat and why is your heart sad? Am I not better to you than ten sons?" Translate: You've got me and a double-portion of food—what more do you want? How did Hannah handle his insensitivity (1:9–10)?

4. What marriage trouble is brewing when the home becomes more child-centered than spouse-centered?

Follow-up: With two or three kids in tow, it's hard to fan the flames of romance. What practical suggestions can you make that will help younger couples keep their relationship in balance and grow their marital commitment?

5. Sometimes our focus on prayer is polite prayer, tame prayer, folded hands prayer. Read the prayers of Scripture—these people approached God with boldness and passion. Like Hannah. She wept and prayed and pleaded with Heaven, O God, please do not ignore me ... Please, Lord ... I beg you to listen ... One other thing you learn about prayer is this: God honors persistence. It's as if He says, Finally! Finally, you are asking something worthy of My name! Hannah prayed big and bold. One way we bring honor to God is by the size of our requests. He loves it when His people have *big* faith and pray *big* prayers—and refuse to go away. Pray *big* ... Do you?

6. Samuel was born. Hannah lived each day with the realization of her vow. How do you think she was able to follow through on her promise?

7. What if your son wanted to take the message of Christ to a foreign land and live there? Would you be willing to let go and *let God?*

8. Describe the difference Samuel made to Israel. Describe the difference Hannah made to Samuel.

The Amazing Story of Abigail
1 Samuel 25

When Abigail saw David, she hurried and dismounted from her donkey,
and fell on her face before David and bowed herself to the ground.
She fell at his feet and said . . . "Please let your maidservant speak
to you, and listen to the words of your maidservant . . ."
—1 Samuel 25:23–24—

Stories appear regularly of someone finding hidden treasure—a $10 painting at a yard sale that turns out to be a priceless masterpiece, or an old dusty violin that turns out to be handcrafted by Antonio Stradivari. But what if the ones who discovered them didn't care about them? What if the man with the painting didn't like it, rolled it up, and tossed it in the trash? What if the woman had no clue about the violin and merely cast it aside? Such lack of appreciation for value causes us to cringe.

Sadly, such disrespect for value occurs daily and with something of much more importance than paintings and violins. It happens with people.

1 Samuel 25 tells the story of Abigail—a sparkling gem of a treasure. She was a woman of integrity, wisdom, virtue, and beauty. Indeed, she was a woman with worth "far above rubies" (Proverbs 31:10). There was only one problem. She was married to a jerk. Her husband had no concept or appreciation for the priceless treasure he had in a wife. She was an amazing woman with an equally amazing story.

Who can find a virtuous woman?
For her price is far above rubies.
—Proverbs 31:10—

I. The Three Characters in the Story (one hero, one villain, one heroine).

   A. The handsome hero—David. The story begins at the end—the end of one of Israel's greatest leaders. "Then Samuel died" (v. 1). Getting a historical "feel" for the story is essential. Judge Samuel has been the leader in Israel for years. He had already anointed the new king-elect (David) to replace the insane Saul. But now Samuel is dead and David is on the run. Saul became so jealous of David that he had lost touch with reality. He pursued David relentlessly.

      1. In the previous chapter, David encountered Saul in a cave although the king had no idea David was anywhere around. David could have killed his nemesis and immediately proclaimed himself the new "King!" But that would involve vengeance and running ahead of God. David withdrew and refused to lay a hand on "the Lord's anointed" (24:6–7).

      2. Hurray for David! Later when Saul discovered David's mercy, he was so taken aback by David's grace that he called off the manhunt. The result: David and his men were left to roam the wilderness and scratch out a living (25:1b).

      3. However, rather than become desperadoes, David and his men employed themselves as a wilderness police force. They protected ranchers and shepherds from the danger of the open range (wild animals, poachers, or bandits). There was no need for formal contracts to be signed. It merely became customary in those days for ranchers to pay a percentage of profits to those who protected their investment from loss. Only a fool would refuse to acknowledge the work of David and his men.

   B. The foolish villain—Nabal, 25:2–3a. The name "Nabal" means foolish one. It was fitting. Here was a man who was vulgar, belligerent, selfish, and stubborn. He was not the kind of man you wanted to work for (or be married to).

    C. The beautiful heroine—Abigail, v. 3. For everything that Nabal wasn't, she was! The most remarkable aspect of Abigail was that she retained her dignity in spite of her husband's foolishness. She brought integrity, honor, and commitment to a tough marriage. By the way, if you want an example of God at work in homes that aren't all they should be, this is the story for you.

II. The Plot.

    A. Request for Payment. For months David's men had been voluntarily watching over Nabal's sizeable investment. When word reached David that Nabal was shearing his sheep in order to market the wool, David knew it was time to collect his gratuity (vv. 4–5). David instructs his men not to be pushy or demanding of a specific amount, but to be gracious in their approach (vv. 6–9). Give us whatever you think is fair.

        1. You can see the smirk on Nabal's face (vv. 10–11). "Who is David? Shall I take my bread and my water and my meat that I have slaughtered for my shearers, and give it to men whose origin I do not know?" Translate: *Everyone's looking for a handout these days. Get lost!*

        2. Note: it would have been impossible for Nabal not to know who David was (his wife certainly knew).

        3. David's men returned and reported Nabal's refusal (v. 12).

    B. "Vengeance is Mine!" said David. Nabal is stingy, and David is seething. Although he had previously reined in his vengeance in the previous chapter (remember the cave at Engedi?), David's wrath exploded (v. 13).

        1. What happened to the cool, calm, and collected David who was willing to let the Lord fight his battles? Why isn't David praying about this? Why isn't he leaving vengeance in the hands of the One to whom it belongs?

        2. One of the greatest lessons to be learned is this: you cannot live today on yesterday's obedience. Suddenly,

David throws caution to the wind and gives the order: *Come on boys—gird on your sword and let's ride!*

3. David is feeling justified. He's also mouthing as he rides: *This isn't fair! I have every right to be paid! We have given him weeks of man-hours and work, and he hasn't lost a single sheep! I'm tired of being taken advantage of—No more!*

C. Meanwhile back at the ranch: Word reaches Abigail of her husband's foolishness as a servant implores her to do something—and quick (vv. 14–17). "He [Nabal] is such a worthless man that no one can speak to him." No one knew the truth of those words better than did Abigail.

1. Put yourself in her place. She has been putting up with an ungrateful husband for years. Finally, this was her chance. How tempting it would have been to slip off in the back room with a smile and a prayer that said, *Oh well. May the Lord's will be done.*

2. She refuses. In fact, her integrity rises to the occasion. Rather than thinking that her husband would get what he deserved, she is more concerned about the new king-elect and his reputation! She must move fast to save David from doing something that would hurt his influence for years to come.

3. The question she ponders is the same one you must ponder in any situation: *What would the Lord have me to do?* She doesn't excuse her husband nor does she enable him. Instead, she was willing to turn matters over to God. She would protect "the Lord's anointed"—as David had done previously re: Saul.

III. The Plan.

Talk about a Proverbs 31 kind of woman! Within minutes of assessing the situation, she engages in an ingenious plan to save her husband's life and David's reputation. She organizes a full-scale catering service for four hundred men. It was the first meals-on-wheels (or hooves).

A. Her intercession, vv. 18–20. What could be the only thing that could stop an angry posse of four hundred men riding full bore? How about this: a beautiful woman with a leg of lamb buffet! By the way, David is seething the entire way (vv. 21–22). Suddenly he rounds a bend and there she is.

1. Her loyalty (vv. 24–25). She falls at David's feet and begs for mercy from the soon-to-be king. She knew Nabal was folly and knew he was deserving of David's anger. However, this was not about Nabal. This was about David—and David's God.

2. Her faith (vv. 26–31a). Don't do this, David! Don't come to the throne with murder on your hands! Yes, you have been wronged, but this is not the answer! Leave vengeance where it belongs—in the hands of God.

3. Her simple request. "When the Lord deals well with my lord, then remember your maidservant," (v. 31b). I don't know how all of this will work out, but it will . . . And when it does, I hope you will remember me.

B. An amazing conclusion . . . She awaits David's response (vv. 32–35). David's heart softened as he recognized the providential hand of God. The king-elect was still teachable and touchable. Disaster averted. Abigail returns home into the arms of a grateful husband. Not quite.

1. She came home to find her husband feasting like a king—so much so that he was drunk with wine (v. 36). Undoubtedly she went to bed alone, weary, and wounded in heart—wondering what it must be like to have a husband who appreciated her. She didn't get angry nor did she storm out of the room. She just went to bed. She had pleaded with David to leave things in the hands of God and now she must do the same.

2. She told him the next morning (v. 37). Regardless of whether he had a heart attack or stroke ("his heart died

within him"), ten days later "the Lord struck Nabal and he died" (v. 38).

3. The lesson cannot be missed: do what is right and leave the rest in the hands of God. He is perfectly capable of handling everything in His time and in His way. You have to believe that and you have to trust Him to do that. And, by the way, if you think this is amazing, wait until you read the rest of the story—*1 Samuel 25:39–42.*

Discussion Questions
Prompting Additional Insight

1. Read 1 Samuel 24. What impresses you about David's restraint?

2. Give a one-word description of Nabal.

3. How is Abigail's example a real-life application of 1 Peter 3:1–2?

4. Were David's men overbearing or demanding of Nabal (vv. 5–9)? What was Nabal's response? What was the response of David's men in verse 12?

5. What disappoints you about David in verse 13?

6. Why do you think Abigail wasn't willing to let things play out on their own? In other words, whatever will be, will be.

Follow-up: How does answering the question: What would the Lord have me to do? Simplify areas of decision-making? Discuss specific steps we can take to ascertain His will and learn life-wisdom that will keep us on track.

7. Discuss Abigail's wise plan of action that would protect the king-elect from murder. And discuss her humble words of wisdom that she offered to David (vv. 24–31).

8. What in this chapter reveals yet another reason why David was "a man after God's own heart"?

9. Discuss the wound in Abigail's heart when she returned home and found her husband drunk. How did she handle it and what advice would you give a woman today who faces a similar situation—living with an ungrateful husband?

10. Think about the questions:

    Do you have any Nabal's in your life?
    People Satan uses to get under your skin and nudge you into sin.
    Do you have any Abigail's in your life?
    People you need to cherish and not take for granted.
    Do you have any David's in your life?
    People whose hearts are humble enough to listen and wise enough to change.

Lesson 9
The Amazing Story of Esther
The Book of Esther

Pure and undefiled religion in the sight of God our Father is this: to visit the orphans and widows in their distress (James 1:27). That single Bible verse has haunted me for years—along with 1 John 3:18, "Let us not love with word or with tongue, but in deed and truth." Translate: *Put your money, time, and energy where your faith is!*

Truthfully, I haven't always known how to go about fulfilling that admonition. What? Where? Who?—do I trust? Sometimes the mind becomes so numb to the overwhelming plight of the needy that we decide the best strategy is to do nothing. That's not a good strategy.

Orphans. Adoption. Making the impossible become a reality. Perhaps we need to be reminded:

- Jesus was adopted! While conceived miraculously in the womb of Mary, Jesus was adopted into the heart of Joseph. Jesus grew up in the carpentry shop under the feet of His adopted father long before He ever became a preacher.
- Moses was adopted! In an amazing story of God's providence, he was actually adopted twice: by the daughter of Pharaoh and then by his own mother who gladly took on a nanny role.
- Samuel was adopted! Hannah prayed earnestly for a child with the promise that she would give him back to the Lord. She did. For all practical purposes, Samuel was raised by the priest Eli in the shadow of the tabernacle.
- You are adopted! It's easy to forget that. Romans 8:15—"For you have all received a spirit of adoption as sons by which we cry out, 'Abba! Father!'" If you are a Christian, you are a child of God by adoption.

Consider one more amazing story of adoption:

Esther—the adopted orphan who became queen!

"He was bringing up Hadassah, that is Esther,
his uncle's daughter, for she had no father or mother."
—Esther 2:7—

I. The Biography of Adoption.
    Esther was a young Jewish orphan who was mercifully adopted by
    her cousin Mordecai. The drama surrounding her life involves the
    following characters:
    •   Ahasuerus, king of Persia
    •   Vashti, the queen
    •   Haman, the anti-Semitic villain.
    Note: Esther is the only book in the Bible that doesn't mention
    the name of God. However, even though His name is not
    mentioned, the footprints of His providence are everywhere.
    Replete with riveting drama, this ancient story of adoption
    continues to speak today.

II. Beautiful, Bold, and Filled with Courage.
    A. A Drunken Feast Marked by Self-Respect—chapter 1. The
        story begins with the king throwing a huge party for the
        capital city (1:5). During the seven days of unlimited show-off
        revelry, "the royal wine was plentiful" (v. 7). On the seventh
        day when the king's heart was especially festive, he sent for
        Queen Vashti to parade her beauty in front of his drunken
        guests (vv. 10-11). She refused to come.
        1. While many women would applaud her self-respect,
            the king was embarrassed and angry (vv. 12–15). The
            monarch who could command a nation could not
            command his wife. Concerned that her actions might
            influence other Persian wives to disobey their husbands,
            the king's advisors "advised" that he ban her from his
            presence, dethrone her as queen, and replace her with one
            more deserving (vv. 16–20).

2. "This word pleased the king" (vv. 21–22).

B. The New Miss Persia—chapter 2. To replace the banished queen, the king stages a beauty pageant. It comes as no surprise that Esther is chosen and taken to Susa. Concerned for her safety in an anti-Semitic environment, her adoptive cousin, Mordecai, warns her not to reveal her Jewish identity. God's providential hand lands squarely on Esther (2:17) setting up the drama to come.

C. Hitler Wasn't the First—chapter 3. Haman is appointed second in command, and the citizenry is commanded to bow before him (vv. 1–2). Everyone bowed except Mordecai (v. 2b). As a devout Jew, Mordecai would not bow in homage to anyone but God (v. 4). Haman was furious and concocted an ego-driven holocaust against Mordecai and his people (vv. 5–6). He made his appeal to the king by declaring that "it is not in the king's interest to let them remain" (vv. 8–9). Content with Haman's assessment and wishing to stop rebellion against his authority, the king handed the Jews over to Haman to "do with them as you please" (vv. 10–11).

D. One Amazing Woman—chapter 4. After discovering Haman's plot, Mordecai and his people mourned "loudly and bitterly" (v. 1). When word reaches Queen Esther, she seeks details but stops short of offering any real help (vv. 4–12). It is then that Mordecai sends her a convicting message that serves as the key verse in the book. Verse 14: *If you remain silent at this time, relief and deliverance will arise for the Jews from another place and you and your father's house will perish. And who knows whether you have attained royalty for such a time as this?* Mordecai sees the hand of divine providence at work and calls upon his cousin to act with courage. Esther gets it. She is willing to take the risk (vv. 15–17).

E. A Collision Course—chapter 5. Risking her life, Esther appears in the king's presence uninvited (a serious breech of Persian protocol). She is relieved when he welcomes her and beckons her to make request (vv. 1–3). Oddly enough, she invites the king and Haman to a special dinner she has prepared (v. 4). Later, when asked by the king about her request, she mysteriously invites them to a second dinner the following day (vv. 5-8).

1. Haman is swelled up with pride. Not only is he the right hand man to the most powerful potentate in the world, but now he is so important that he is invited to the private dinners of the king and queen.

2. His ego quickly deflates when he sees Mordecai refusing to bow (v. 9). Enraged, Haman orders a gallows built upon which he would hang Mordecai the next day (vv. 9–14).

F. A Providential Twist—chapter 6. Meanwhile . . . The king couldn't sleep and ordered that his chronicles be read to him (v. 1). Out of all the possible "chronicles," it was read to the king how a man named Mordecai had alerted the palace of an assassination attempt (v. 2; 2:21–23). What did we ever do for him? When King Ahasuerus learned that "nothing" had been done, he set out to honor Mordecai (v. 3).

1. At that moment Haman appeared in the court in order to obtain the royal signature on Mordecai's death decree (v. 4). Before Haman could say anything, Ahasuerus asks his second in command: "What is to be done for the man whom the king desires to honor?" Certain that the king would not want to honor anyone but him, Haman gives it his best (vv. 6–9). I would put him in the king's robes, place him on the king's horse, and parade him through the city proclaiming his honor. The king agreed and said, I want you to do it for Mordecai!

2. Haman was mortified (vv. 10–12). He hurried home to even more bad news (v. 14).

G. Poetic justice—chapter 7. When the king asks Esther again regarding her request, she spoke without hesitation (vv. 3–4). Outraged, the king demands to know the one responsible for such a diabolical scheme (v. 5). Esther replied, "A foe and an enemy is this wicked Haman!" It's no surprise that the chapter ends with Haman hanging on the gallows he had built for Mordecai (vv. 9–10).

III. For Such a Time As This.
    A.   Haman's plot to destroy the Jews is foiled because of Esther—an adopted woman who courageously risked her life to save her people. The story closes with the promotion of Mordecai (8:1–2) and a plan for the Jews to defend themselves before any aggressors (vv. 11–17).
    B.   Lest the day of scheduled annihilation become a bitter anniversary on the Jewish calendar, God turned it into a celebration (9:20–32). On that day and to this day, the Jewish people stop and remember the orphan who saved a nation. It remains a custom for the book of Esther to be read in Jewish synagogues on the eve of the feast of Purim.

And all the accomplishments of his authority and strength, and the full account of the greatness of Mordecai to which the king advanced him, are they not written in the Book of the Chronicles of the Kings of Media and Persia? For Mordecai the Jew was second only to King Ahasuerus, and great among the Jews and in favor with his many kinsmen, one who sought the good of his people and one who spoke for the welfare of his whole nation. (Esther 10:2–3)

Discussion Questions
Prompting Additional Insight

1.   Adoption. Mordecai adopted Esther and raised her as his own. Discuss how physical adoption mirrors our own spiritual adoption (Ephesians 1:5; Romans 8:15).

2. Joseph of Nazareth—Joseph is not Jesus' biological father (not a trace of Joseph's DNA could be found in the dried blood of Jesus from the wood of the cross), but he was his earthly father (Luke 2:41, 48). People in the first century knew how babies were conceived. That's why when Mary tells Joseph that she is pregnant, he isn't exactly excited about it. That's when God intervened (Matthew 1:18–24). Joseph walked away from his reputation—"Poor Joseph: he got hoodwinked by *that* girl"—and took care of Mary. And when he took Mary and the child and fled to Egypt because of Herod, it meant he walked away from economic security. We forget about Joseph and the sacrifices he made. Then, again, adoption isn't charity, it is spiritual warfare. Discuss.

3. James 1:27 has always haunted me. Certainly not everyone can adopt a child (nor should they). However, when we encourage a culture of adoption, we are picturing something that's true about God—Hosea 14:3, "For in You the orphan finds mercy." Discuss how Christians can fulfill this admonition in a supportive role for families who can adopt.

4. Sadly, human history is riddled with the corpses of children. In what way was Haman, Pharaoh, Herod, and Hitler the Planned Parenthood of their day?

5. What inspires you the most about the story of Esther?

6. Discuss God's providence. How did it work in the life of Esther? How has it worked in your own life?

What if a mighty battalion of Christian parents would open their hearts and homes to unwanted children—those who escaped the abortionist's knife or the orphanage's grip—to find at your knee the grace of a carpenter's Son? I'm seeing more and more Christians adopting and others rallying in support of their decision to do so. For more information, I recommend the book, *Adopted for Life* by Russell D. Moore. And if you are serious about adoption or know someone who is, I recommend the group: Sacred Selections. They have changed our lives.

www.sacredselections.org
(916) 770–0336

Lesson 10

The Amazing Story of Mary

Matthew 1—2; Luke 1:26—2:52

The angel Gabriel was sent from God to a city in Galilee called Nazareth, to a virgin engaged to a man whose name was Joseph, of the descendants of David; and the virgin's name was Mary. And coming in, he said to her, "Greetings, favored one! The Lord is with you."
—Luke 1:26–28—

From all the women ever born, an obscure Galilean girl named Mary was chosen to bring the Savior into the world. Her greatest tragedy, however, is not of her own doing, but is the product of an apostasy by which man elevated her to a position of worship she never sought.

Mary has been given godlike status. Thousands bow before her statues or are taught to pray to her and through her—as if she is more approachable than Jesus Himself. The Roman Catholic Church has advanced various religious doctrines about Mary which have no basis in Scripture: (1) her sinlessness, (2) her perpetual virginity, (3) her bodily assumption into heaven, and (4) her co-redemptrix with Christ. In fact, it is quite common to find many who believe she makes modern-day appearances.

- In 2004, a grilled cheese sandwich was sold on eBay for $28,000 when it was thought the image of Mary was burned into the toast.
- In Chicago a shrine exists beneath a freeway underpass where it is believed the image of Mary resides in salt stains in the wall.
- Pope Paul II dedicated his papal reign to Mary, embroidered an "M" on his papal garments, prayed to her, and left the care of the Catholic Church to Mary in his will.

Sometimes it seems the homage paid to Mary is more than to Mary's Son. It is something Mary never sought.

The Bible debunks the Maryology teachings of the Catholic Church. Revelation 19:10 tells us that God is the Only One worthy of worship. The closest the New Testament comes to the worship of Mary is Luke 11:27—to which Jesus replies with a rebuke. Mary was not sinless. She calls God her "Savior" in Luke 1:47. God only saves those who are lost (Rom.3:23). Her "perpetual virginity" is answered in Matthew 13:55–56a.

Mary was an average girl of common means from a poor town in Galilee where she was engaged to a blue-collar carpenter. If you had met Mary on the street you probably wouldn't have noticed her. However, God did notice her. And the story surrounding her is absolutely *amazing*.

I. Mary's Heritage.
    A. The Genealogy. Luke gives her genealogy (3:23–38) while Matthew's account records Joseph's (1:1–16). Both Joseph and Mary descended from David and prior to David they shared common ancestry. Mary's branch of the family came through David's son, Nathan, while Joseph's side came through Solomon. Thus, Jesus could lay legal claim to David via Joseph and blood claim through His mother, Mary.
    B. The Announcement (that changed her life), Luke 1:26–27. The name "Mary" is the equivalent of the Hebrew "Miriam." We are told that Mary had a sister who stood with her at the crucifixion (John 19:25). Mary was also related to Elizabeth—the mother of John the Baptist (Luke 1:36).
        1. Mary's age at the time of the visit from the angel Gabriel is unknown. It was customary in those days for a girl to be betrothed while young (perhaps a teen) as marriages were often arranged by parents. It was at this time that she was engaged to a man named Joseph who is called a "righteous man" (Matthew 1:19).
        2. Scripture makes clear that Mary was a "virgin" when Jesus was conceived by the Holy Spirit (Luke 1:27). The specific

Greek term used for "virgin" allows for no other meaning.

3. It was customary for couples to be "betrothed" for one year, and it was as binding as the marriage itself. The couple would live apart with no physical relations. One of the purposes of the betrothal period was to demonstrate moral fidelity (vv. 31, 34–35).

4. The angelic announcement was costly to Mary as the stigma of unwed pregnancy was great. Joseph assumed the worst and was ready to put her away (Matthew 1:18–20). Mary, aware of the cost, surrendered herself unconditionally (Luke 1:38). There is no evidence that she ever brooded over the consequences to her reputation. Instead, she humbly submitted.

II. Mary's Response of Worship.

A. Elizabeth's prophecy, Luke 1:39–45. The angel told Mary additional exciting news: her relative (probably her aunt) Elizabeth, although of advanced age and barren, was also expecting a child (Luke 1:36). Mary immediately rushed to Elizabeth's home where there was mutual rejoicing (vv. 39–40). Nothing indicates that Mary had sent word of her circumstances ahead to Elizabeth. Rather, Elizabeth's knowledge of Mary's condition came by revelation of the Holy Spirit (v. 41). Elizabeth's message (vv. 42–45) was prophetic. "Blessed are you among women, and blessed is the fruit of your womb!" Indeed.

B. Mary's prophecy, Luke 1:46–55. Mary replies with an outpouring of poetic praise to the God who had blessed her. Her prayer of joy is similar to that spoken by Hannah (1 Samuel 2:1–10). Perhaps those who venerate Mary should re-read her praise. God is the One Mary magnifies. She praises Him for His power, mercy, holiness, glory, and faithfulness. She is consumed by the wonder of His grace. She pondered . . . How could a holy God do such a great thing to one as undeserving as am I?

III. Her Relationship with Her Son.

    A. Three scenes. Mary appears three times during the ministry of Jesus.

        1. *At the wedding in Cana of Galilee, John 2.* When the wine ran out at the wedding reception, Mary knew that Jesus had the ability to solve it (vv. 1–3). While Jesus' response seems disrespectful when translated into English (v. 4), it carried a different connotation then. His intent was not to wound, but to correct and instruct. Mary's earthly role as mother did not give her the right to manage His God-appointed mission. As a man, He was her son. But as God, He was her Lord. Jesus did respond with a miracle, but not because of His mother. He worked a miracle because the time had come (v. 11).

        2. *At Capernaum, Mark 3.* When Jesus is beset by large crowds, His family is concerned about His safety (vv. 31–35). Jesus sends the same message again. His earthly relatives laid no claim to His spiritual mission. Neither His mother nor His brothers would be allowed to call the shots. They would have to submit to His Lordship like everyone else. *Note:* Mary never appears again except in the background. She would never usurp her role. How foolish to think that she does so today!

        3. *At the cross.* The last time we see Mary in the gospel accounts is when she sees her firstborn crucified on a cross like a common thief. There are no words to express what was happening in Mary's heart that day.

    B. The sword that pierced her soul. She knew this day would come. As an infant, Joseph and Mary took Jesus to Jerusalem to dedicate Him at the temple (Luke 2:21ff). While there they met an elderly man named Simeon (vv. 25–26) who spoke prophetically about both Jesus and Mary.

And Simeon blessed them and said to Mary His mother, "Behold, this Child is appointed for the fall and rise of many in Israel, and

*for a sign to be opposed—and a sword will pierce even your own
soul . . ." (vv. 34–35).*

1. Author Luke undoubtedly interviewed Mary for he states
   in the beginning of his historical narrative that he sought
   out those who were "eyewitnesses." Thus the mother of
   Jesus would have been one of those eyewitnesses as he
   describes events about which only she would have known.
2. Years later she would watch as a Roman soldier thrust a
   sword into the side of her Son and, in so doing, into her
   own soul as well. Certainly she remembered the old man's
   prophecy.
3. Mary had to live with the horror of watching Jesus die—of
   hearing the taunts and insults. No one knew Jesus more
   than she did. No one loved Jesus more than she did. The
   pain of her grief on that awful Friday is unimaginable. Yet
   she was there and stayed unto the end. She was clearly a
   woman of grace and dignity.
4. Jesus' last earthly act before dying was to make sure Mary
   received proper care. Without a doubt, the apostle John
   did exactly as He was asked.

*When Jesus then saw His mother, and the disciple whom He
loved standing nearby, He said to His mother, "Woman, behold
your son!" Then he said to the disciple, "Behold your mother!"
From that hour the disciple took her into his own household.
(John 19:26–27)*

Conclusion

Mary was unlike any other mother. Godly mothers typically are
absorbed in training up their children to go to heaven. Mary's Son
was the Lord of heaven. The last we see of her is in Acts 1:14 when she
is in the company of the disciples after Jesus had ascended back to
heaven. She is never mentioned again.

Mary is not once mentioned in the epistles. Mary is never mentioned as an object of veneration by the early church. She would be appalled to learn that she has become the object of worship. A humble woman, she always pointed away from self and toward Her Son and Savior, Jesus. What an amazing story!

Discussion Questions
Prompting Additional Insight

1. What comes to mind when you hear the name of Mary, the mother of Jesus?

2. Do you think we talk enough about her? Why or why not?

3. The angel's message was puzzling to this young girl from backwoods Galilee. With the promise that she would "conceive in her womb and bear a child" –what was her reaction (Luke 1:34)? What is the angel's answer (v. 35)? What is Mary's reply (v. 38)? What does that tell you about God's reason for choosing her?

4. Lost in the shuffle of events surrounding the birth announcement of Jesus is the character of Joseph. Read Matthew's account (1:18-25) and discuss Joseph's reaction and the kind of man he was.

5. Her early days with a new baby was a whirlwind of activity: a stable for a delivery room, the visit of the shepherds telling about an angelic encounter, the prophecy of Simeon . . . Later there would be the visit of the Magi and their talk of a guiding star, Herod's jealous plan to kill their child and the angelic command: "Get up! Take the Child and . . . flee to Egypt . . . " and their eventual return to Nazareth. Nothing about this had been easy.

During it all, however, Mary never wavered in her faith. She simply trusted. What is the lesson for us?

6. Watching Jesus grow . . . Other than the temple incident at age twelve when He became separated from them (which produced some anxious moments—Great! God gave me His Son and I've lost Him!)— nothing is revealed about His childhood except this: "And His mother treasured all these things in her heart" (Luke 2:51). Mothers do that. As a mom, what are the things you treasure in your heart as you watch your children grow?

7. Think about the following questions for Mary:
    —Did you ever feel awkward teaching Him about God?
    —How did He respond when He saw a lamb being led to slaughter?
    —How did He act at funerals?
    —When someone mentioned Satan, what did He say?
    —Did you and Joseph ever consider that God was living in your house?
    —What were you thinking when you watched Him die?
    —What question would you like to ask Mary?

Lesson 11

The Amazing Story of Mary & Martha

Luke 10:38–42

Mary was seated at the Lord's feet, listening to His word.
But Martha was distracted with all her preparations . . .
—Luke 10:39–40—

Taking a detour from our studies of individual women, we'll look at these two together—because that's how Scripture presents them. They shared a home with their brother, Lazarus, about two miles from Jerusalem in the village of Bethany. It was here that Jesus found a parenthesis of peace in His Judean travels thanks to the hospitality of these siblings.

Mary and Martha were an interesting pair—very different in some ways—very similar in others. One thing however is obvious: both of them were devoted to Jesus and He to them. "Now Jesus loved Martha and her sister and Lazarus" (John 11:5).

We do not know how they struck up a relationship. It's quite possible they were among those who heard Jesus teach publicly and became followers. At some point they extended hospitality to Him and He accepted. It transitioned into a warm and personal friendship, and their home became a place where Jesus could find respite among the hectic events surrounding His Jerusalem visits.

Hospitality was the hallmark of this family. The Bethany home belonged to Martha (Luke 10:38) which may be indicative that she was the elder sister. Scripture doesn't say if any of them had been married nor does it give their ages. What we do know is that they welcomed Jesus into their home and that He was clearly made to feel "at home" among these special friends.

Mary and Martha—Two sisters who used their unique gifts in different ways while providing some amazing snapshots into the ministry of Jesus.

I.   Three Scenes in Bethany.
    A. Luke 10:38–42—The first scene depicts a clash of temperaments over how best to show their devotion to Jesus. Martha was the devoted servant who seemed to be fussing over her hostess duties. She was conscientious and considerate and wanted everything to be just right. It was one thing to entertain guests; it was quite another to host the Son of God.
        1. Much of Martha's behavior is commendable. And unless I miss my guess, most women would be sympathetic toward Martha. After all, it would border on rude to do all the work while your sister sits around chatting with guests. Thus Martha goes about her business preparing a meal for Jesus all the while growing irritated that Mary was no where to be found.
        2. One wonders if Martha made "subtle" hints that she needed help. Did she bang a few pots and pans and make extra noise in the kitchen as an SOS for some assistance? Did she clear her throat or seek to catch her sister's eye when she came into the room? We don't know. At some point we do know that she gave up any pretense of subtlety and aired her grievance against Mary in front of Jesus—asking Him to intervene by ordering her into the kitchen.
        3. Jesus' reply to Martha was unexpected. It never occurred to her that she could be the one needing correction. Jesus overlooked her implication of accusation against Him ("Lord, do You not care . . .") and offered a rebuke that was gentle yet pointed.
        4. Thus Jesus commends Mary for focusing on the critical priority of the moment. Listening and worshiping should

always take precedent over busyness and doing. With the best of intentions, Martha's conscientious attention to serving was commendable. However, her self-focus and resentment of Mary's devotion was not. "Martha, Martha, you are worried and bothered by so many things; but only one thing is necessary, for Mary has chosen the good part, which shall not be taken away from her."

B. John 11—The raising of Lazarus had a profound impact on both sisters while illustrating the difference in their personalities. Although their words are similar, their posture is not. When Jesus finally arrives, Martha runs to Him while Mary remained in the house (v. 20). Note the similarity of their initial greetings in verse 21 and verse 32: *Martha:* "Lord, if You had been here, my brother would not have died." *Mary:* "Lord, if You had been here, my brother would not have died."

1. Their response to Jesus indicates previous and similar discussions among themselves. But note the difference: Martha needed intellectual support (vv. 21–27) while Mary needed emotional support (vv. 32–36).

2. Martha needed to know that Jesus was in control; Mary needed to know that Jesus cared. Without rebukes or reservations, Jesus met each sister where she was— whether standing or falling prostrate at His feet; whether needing intellectual support or emotional reassurance.

3. More than any other act of Jesus, the raising of Lazarus would be the miracle that would seal the Jewish leaders determination to put Him to death (vv. 45–53). The two sisters were certainly aware of the "talk" around town and the threat against Jesus. They would have to know that by raising their brother from the dead, Jesus placed His own life in peril. All of which makes the next scene so poignant.

C. John 12—Amidst the swirl of Jewish controversy over the raising of Lazarus and as an expression of gratitude, knowing that Jesus had risked His own life by giving Lazarus back his,

Mary anoints the feet of Jesus and wipes His feet with her hair (vv. 1–3). It was an act of humble devotion. Her action was a reenactment of a similar anointing by someone else earlier in His ministry (Luke 7:36–50). It was Mary's way of signifying how much she loved Him.

1. Jesus willingly accepted her offering (Matthew 26:6–13; Mark 14:3–9). This time, however, it was Judas who complained about Mary's devotion to Jesus (John 12:4–5). From his question it appears he was seeking to elicit support for such wastefulness. This time Martha held her peace. Although she is again seen serving (v. 2), she no longer seems resentful of Mary's attention to Jesus.

2. Both sisters loved Jesus deeply although each expressed their devotion in different ways. One thing is clear: Jesus loved them back with the deepest of affection (John 11:5).

II. Three Questions We Must Answer.

A. Are we placing preference of self above Jesus? In the Luke 10 scene, Martha's behavior seems at first to be the mark of genuine servanthood. After all, she was the one who put on the apron and went to work serving her guests—including Jesus. Her subsequent treatment of Mary and harsh words toward Jesus, however, betrayed a heart defect.

1. "Lord, do You not care that my sister has left me to do all the serving alone? Tell her to help me." Martha was wrong in her judgment of Mary. Mary wasn't being lazy or inhospitable. Truthfully, it was Mary whose heart was in the right place. And Jesus knew it. He knew it because He knew the hearts of both women.

2. Martha had allowed the busyness of the moment to rob her of what should have been the primary focus of her heart: listening to Jesus. Her initial question to Him betrayed her heart condition: "Lord, do You not care?" Did she really think that Jesus didn't care? Certainly she knew better. But for the moment she had lost her focus.

Rather than focusing first on Jesus, she focused first on self. Hence, "Martha, Martha, you are so worried and bothered about so many things . . ."

3. In contrast, Mary was so consumed with the opportunity to sit at the feet of Jesus that, for the moment, nothing else mattered. Worshiping Him and listening to Him was the 100% focus of her energies. So it must be with ours.

B. Have we found the one thing? "But only one thing is necessary, for Mary has chosen the good part." What is the one thing? This is obviously more than telling Martha to limit her menu (although it could have had a double meaning). Jesus seems to be saying that Mary had found the singular focus of life: listening to Jesus and responding to His word. Everything else is secondary. It's not that Martha's attention to service wasn't important; it was that Mary's undivided devotion to Christ was more important. Like the promise offered to Mary is the promise offered to all who choose the "one thing." "It will not be taken away." Keep your life-focus on Christ and Him crucified (Paul's one thing, 1 Corinthians 2:1–2) and you will be rewarded.

C. Are we focusing more on service or on worship? Jesus told the Samaritan woman that God seeks "true worshipers" (John 4:23). He truly found one in Mary.

1. It's easy for our busyness (even spiritual busyness AKA "church work") to eclipse the devotion of our worship. As a result, if we aren't careful we can know all about the Lord and never stop long enough to know Him. That happens when we focus more on what we can do for Christ and less upon remembering what He has done for us. The former promotes actions of busyness (which may be right within themselves) while the latter promotes times of introspection, reflection, and worship.

2. It's not that works of faith are not important (any more than Martha's attention to serving her guests was not important—it was!); it's just that worship is more

important. It's a matter of priorities. Here it is: *get the first one right and the others will follow.*

Martha loved Jesus, and her faith was real. It's important to know that. She had allowed herself, however, to become spiritually unbalanced. Jesus' kind words of reproof serve as a reminder to all of us. Worship is the one thing most needed. Actions of faith must always flow through that and be subordinate to that. The Pharisees never understood that distinction and, as a result, went through the motions of religion while never engaging the heart.

Mary and Martha: different and yet so much alike. *An amazing story!*

Discussion Questions
Prompting Additional Insight

1. Why do we tend to take "Martha's side" when she was aggravated with her sister?

2. What do you think drew Jesus to their home? Would He be drawn to yours?

3. Read between the lines of Martha's rebuke of Mary (Luke 10:40)? What tells you that she had lost her focus?

4. Discuss the difference seen in the two sisters in the John 11 scene when Jesus arrives after the death of Lazarus?

5. What was Martha doing in John 12:1–2? What did Mary do that earned the rebuke of Judas (vv. 3–5)? What did Martha say about

Mary's distraction/devotion on that occasion? What lesson(s) can we learn?

6. "Practice hospitality" (Romans 12:13). In our busy times we have dismissed this admonition with the excuse, "Hospitality means more than having people in your home." Okay, that's true. Here's a question: Wouldn't a part of hospitality include having people in your home? Discuss the excuses for why we fail to open our homes and share our blessings with others.

   Follow-up—What is the real meaning of hospitality?

7. The story of the two sisters is not all that different from women today. Like Mary, you long to sit at the feet of Jesus, but the daily demands of a busy world just won't leave you alone. Like Martha, you love the Lord and serve Him in many ways—teaching a Bible class, taking food to the sick, going to the hospital, writing cards of encouragement, etc. In all of this, however, you struggle with weariness and feelings of inadequacy.

   Then comes Jesus right into the middle of your busy Martha life and extends the same invite He issued long ago. Softly and tenderly He invites you to choose "the better part" –a joyful life of "living room" intimacy that will more naturally turn into "kitchen service" for Him. But how? How do we find time to become a true-worshiper? How do we prioritize and find the "one thing?" Discuss the impact of these women on your life. Are you more of a Mary or more of a Martha?

The Amazing Story of Mary Magdalene

John 20:1–18

*Now after He had risen early on the first day of the week, He appeared
first to Mary Magdalene, from whom He had cast out seven demons.*
—Mark 16:9—

S he is one of the best known yet least understood women of
Scripture. She is mentioned in all four gospel accounts, followed
Jesus to the cross, and has the forever distinction of being the first
witness to His resurrection. Yet the Bible draws a curtain of silence
around much of her life.

Tradition, however, abounds with fictitious stories surrounding Mary
Magdalene. For example:

1. She is identified as the anonymous sinful woman who anointed
   Jesus' feet with perfume (Luke 7:37–38). Yet immediately after
   the scene, Luke introduces us to Mary Magdalene in a completely
   different context with no connection to the previous situation
   (8:1–2). Given Luke's detailed historical chronology, it makes it
   highly unlikely she is the same woman.
2. She is identified as the woman taken in adultery (John 8). Such is
   complete speculation and without any foundation.
3. She is the object of mythological legends. For example, Dan
   Brown's, The DaVinci Code, presents Mary as the secret wife
   of Jesus with whom He had children. Such is blasphemous
   fiction and not biblical reality. Sadly, many are led astray by such
   sensational stories.

Much of what you hear about Mary Magdalene is more hype and
hyperbole than truth. What the Scriptures actually say about her
is amazing enough. There is no need to embellish it with fanciful
speculation.

I. The Darkness of Mary's Life.
   A. Seven demons—Yes, Mary Magdalene had a dark past, but
       it had nothing to do with immorality. Both Mark and Luke
       report that Jesus healed her of demon possession. In fact, she
       had been tormented by "seven demons" (Mark 16:9; Luke
       8:2).
       1. Demon possession appears to be a phenomenon limited
           exclusively to the New Testament era. There is no mention
           of them in the Old Testament. It seems that for a limited
           time God allowed Satan's spirits to possess human beings,
           affecting people both physically and mentally. Likewise, it
           seems plausible to conclude that they were allowed during
           the time of Jesus to prove the Son of God's power over the
           demonic world.
       2. Mark 1:34 presents a clear distinction between demons
           and diseases. Verse 39 shows that the work of Jesus
           consisted of (1) "preaching" and (2) "casting out
           demons." The demons recognized Jesus as the Son of
           God, acknowledged His power, and did not want to have
           anything to do with Him (5:7–8).
       3. One can only imagine the restless torment of agony
           inflicted on Mary by "seven" Satanic demons.
   B. Magdalene—Contrary to what some think, "Magdalene" was
       not her surname or last name. She was called such to
       distinguish her from other "Marys" who followed Jesus.
       In all likelihood, "Magdalene" identified her as being from
       "Magdala"—a city near Capernaum on the northwest shore
       of the Sea of Galilee. It was in this area that Jesus began His
       earthly preaching work. It was also here that He performed
       many miracles—including casting out demons.

II. Her Deliverance and Discipleship.
   A. Set free! Unlike some others (Luke 4:33–37), the specifics
       of Mary's miraculous delivery from the plague of demons are

not given. Undoubtedly, Mary was forever grateful to Jesus. Owing Him everything, she quickly became a disciple.

B. Following Jesus—Luke 8:1–3 report that there were other women traveling with Jesus. How He worked out the logistics of their company isn't stated. First, His honor was at stake. If there was the slightest hint of moral impropriety, the enemies of Jesus would have raised it. They did not.

  1. These women embraced His mission and supported it financially (v. 3b).

  2. Later, when others forsook Him, Mary remained faithful and followed Him all the way to the cross and beyond.

III. Devotion at the Cross.

A. She could not bear to watch nor could she bear to leave. Mary Magdalene is pictured standing with Jesus' mother at the cross. Undoubtedly, she would have been near enough to hear Jesus speak (John 19:25). Mark's account presents the women "looking on from a distance." Perhaps as the gruesomeness of the crucifixion wore on, the women moved back. After all, it was a heart wrenching and emotional scene.

B. After Jesus died, Joseph and Nicodemus obtained permission from Pilate to take the body and wrap it in preparation for burial. They hurried as sundown approached and the Sabbath began.

  1. They carried His body to a new garden tomb "in which no one had yet been laid" (vv. 41–42). They weren't the only ones who witnessed the burial.

  2. Luke 23:55–56 report that the "women who had come with Him out of Galilee followed, and saw the tomb and how His body was laid. Then they returned and prepared spices and perfumes." They would return to the tomb as soon as the Sabbath was over. Although the Sabbath ended at sunset on the seventh day, they must wait for dawn on the first day before they would have enough light to complete the task of anointing the body properly.

IV. Daybreak at the Tomb.

    A. John reports that it was still dark on the first-day morning when Mary Magdalene approached the tomb (20:1). Luke notes that it was "early dawn" (24:1). Mary had no thoughts of resurrection, but only of how she could gain access to the grave. When she found the soldiers gone and the stone rolled away, she immediately concluded that the body had been stolen. She ran for help and breathlessly told Peter and John (John 20:2–6).

        1. The two men ran to the tomb and found it exactly as Mary had reported (vv. 7–10). Confused, dazed, and concluding there was nothing more they could do, the two apostles walked away while Mary stayed.

        2. "But Mary was standing outside the tomb weeping" (v. 11a). Overcome with grief, she "stooped and looked into the tomb" (v. 11b). What she saw next would stay with her the rest of her life. Verse 12: "And she saw two angels in white sitting, one at the head and one at the feet, where the body of Jesus had been lying."

        3. Their question must have been puzzling to her (v. 13). It was then she turned around and saw a man standing behind her. It was Jesus, although His countenance was somehow different (v. 14). She broke down. In between sobs, and supposing He was the garden caretaker, she told Him the reason for her grief.

        4. All He had to do was call her name: "Mary!" Was it the way He said it? Who besides Jesus would even know her name? "Rabboni!" [Teacher] she exclaimed, as she simultaneously reached for Him—clinging with all her might. After an emotional moment, Jesus spoke calmly. "Stop clinging to Me, for I have not yet ascended to My Father." Interestingly enough, He tells believing Mary not to touch Him (hold on to Him). A week later, He insists that unbelieving Thomas reach out and touch Him ("put

your hand into My side" (v. 27). Thomas was afraid to touch Jesus while Mary was afraid to let Him go.

B. Verse 18 reports that she came and announced the incredible news to the apostles: "I have seen the Lord"—and then related what Jesus had spoken to her. It was an amazing morning and one she would never forget.

C. Mary Magdalene was rewarded with unparalleled honor for her unflinching devotion to following Jesus. She was the first one to see and hear Jesus after His resurrection. While the others received word from angels, Mary received word from Jesus Himself. Mark concludes the resurrection scene with these words: "Now after He had risen early on the first day of the week, He first appeared to Mary Magdalene." Mary Magdalene—an *amazing* woman with an *amazing* story.

There you have it—twelve amazing women of Scripture. And there are many more beyond the scope of our study: *Anna*—the elderly faithful witness of Jesus; *The Samaritan woman at the well*—finding her way to the Water of Life; *Lydia*—a hospitable heart opened to the gospel; *Priscilla*—the better half of a married couple who risked their lives for the Cause; and *Dorcas*—abounding in deeds of kindness and love. And then there is the composite "Worthy Woman" of Proverbs 31.

Modern feminism devalues women (while claiming to do the opposite). Christianity, on the other hand, honors women as women and never discounts their intellect, talents, or gifts they bring to the world. The most significant women in Scripture were influential not because of their careers, but because of their character. My Christian sister, may your heart be touched by their faith and may you have their same love for the amazing God they worshiped.

Discussion Questions
Prompting Additional Insight

1. What do you think of when you hear the name: Mary Magdalene?

2. Google Mary Magdalene and the Da Vinci Code. In what ways has the popular book and movie elevated fiction above truth?

3. What did Jesus do for Mary that caused her to be forever thankful?

4. Demon possession—The New Testament draws a clear distinction between demon possession and diseases. Demon possession involved a bondage to an evil spirit of Satan. It appears that they were allowed to afflict people during the earthly walk of Jesus— giving clear evidence of His power over all things evil. Discuss what you learn about demon possession from Mark 5:8–14.

5. According to Luke 8:1–3, how were the women followers of Christ contributing to His ministry?

6. When others walked away from Jesus, Mary stayed by His side. She followed Him all the way from Galilee to Jerusalem; from the cross to the tomb. What does that tell you about Mary and . . . what God seeks from you?

7. What do you conclude about Mary in the following verses:
   —John 19:25
   —John 20:1
   —John 20:10–11
   —John 20:13

8. John 20:14–15—Confused about the empty tomb and the missing body, what question did Mary pose to the "gardener?" How did Jesus finally get her attention?

9. What an honor—Mary Magdalene was the first one to see and hear Jesus post-resurrection (Mark 16:9). What message does that send to us about the appreciation Jesus had for the women who followed and served Him?

10. Out of the women studied, discuss who affected you the most— and be prepared to tell why.